I0803400

NACIONAL
BOSS
MEN'S FASHION
Marlboro

SENNA

THE LEGEND

Bruce Hales-Dutton

sona BOOKS

sona
BOOKS

© Danann Media Publishing Limited 2024

First published in 2018 under the title *Senna: The Illustrated Biography*

Revised edition published in 2024 by Sona Books, an imprint of Danann Media Publishing Limited

WARNING: For private domestic use only, any unauthorised copying, hiring, lending or public performance of this book is illegal.

CAT NO: SON0598

Photography courtesy of

Getty images:

Hoch Zwei/Corbis
Pascal Rondeau
Bob Thomas
Paul-Henri Cahier
Jean-Yves Ruszniewski/Corbis/Vcg
David Madison
Eric Feferberg
Vittoriano Rastelli/Corbis
Kazuhiro Nogi/Afp
Patrick Behar/Corbis
Leo Mason/Popperfoto
Mike Hewitt/Allsport
Gianni Giansanti
Heritage Images
Mike Powell
Mike King
Jean-Marc Loubat
Michael Cooper
Jean-Loup Gautreau
Dario Mitidieri

Other images Alamy. Wiki Commons

Text revisions by Scott Reeves

Cover design Darren Grice at Ctrl-d

Layout design Alex Young at Cre8ive

Editor: Martin Corteel

All rights reserved. No part of this title may be reproduced or transmitted in any material form (including photocopying or storing it in any medium by electronic means and whether or not transiently or incidentally to some other use of this publication) without the written permission of the copyright owner, except in accordance with the provisions of the Copyright, Designs and Patents Act 1988.Applications for the copyright owner's written permission should be addressed to the publisher.

Made in EU.

ISBN: 978-1-915343-57-4

CONTENTS

Ayrton Senna driving the Marlboro McLaren during practice for the Sega European Grand Prix on 10 April 1993

KENWOOD
8
Shell

INTRODUCTION

One evening in the mid-1980s, there was a knock on Alan Potter's front door. On the doorstep was an intense-looking young man who said simply: "John Webb sent me."

In those days, Webb ran Brands Hatch circuit, a piston's toss from Potter's home in Kent. Earlier, Webb had asked his friend Potter if, due to an accommodation shortage, he would be prepared to provide a bed for the night for a driver competing in the forthcoming British Grand Prix. "He came in and went straight up to bed," Potter recalled. "He didn't have anything to eat and we didn't see him until the next morning."

Potter was a keen builder and flyer of model aircraft. The next morning, Potter took his quiet guest into the garden to show him his latest creation: a helicopter. In halting English, the young man asked if he could fly the model. With some trepidation, Potter handed over the precious radio control unit to a man he'd only met the evening before.

The young man's first act was to make adjustments to the engine's mixture control. When he got it running to his liking, he hovered the helicopter close to the ground before suddenly sending it shooting away out of sight. Potter was furious. But then the model returned at the same speed as it departed, still just off the ground.

The guest pilot's next trick was to fly the helicopter on its side with the blades vertical. "It was so close to the ground that the blades were sending up bits of cut grass," Potter recalled. After that the young man called for a plastic

After meeting Alan Potter, Senna had a lifelong interest in model aircraft for the rest of his life

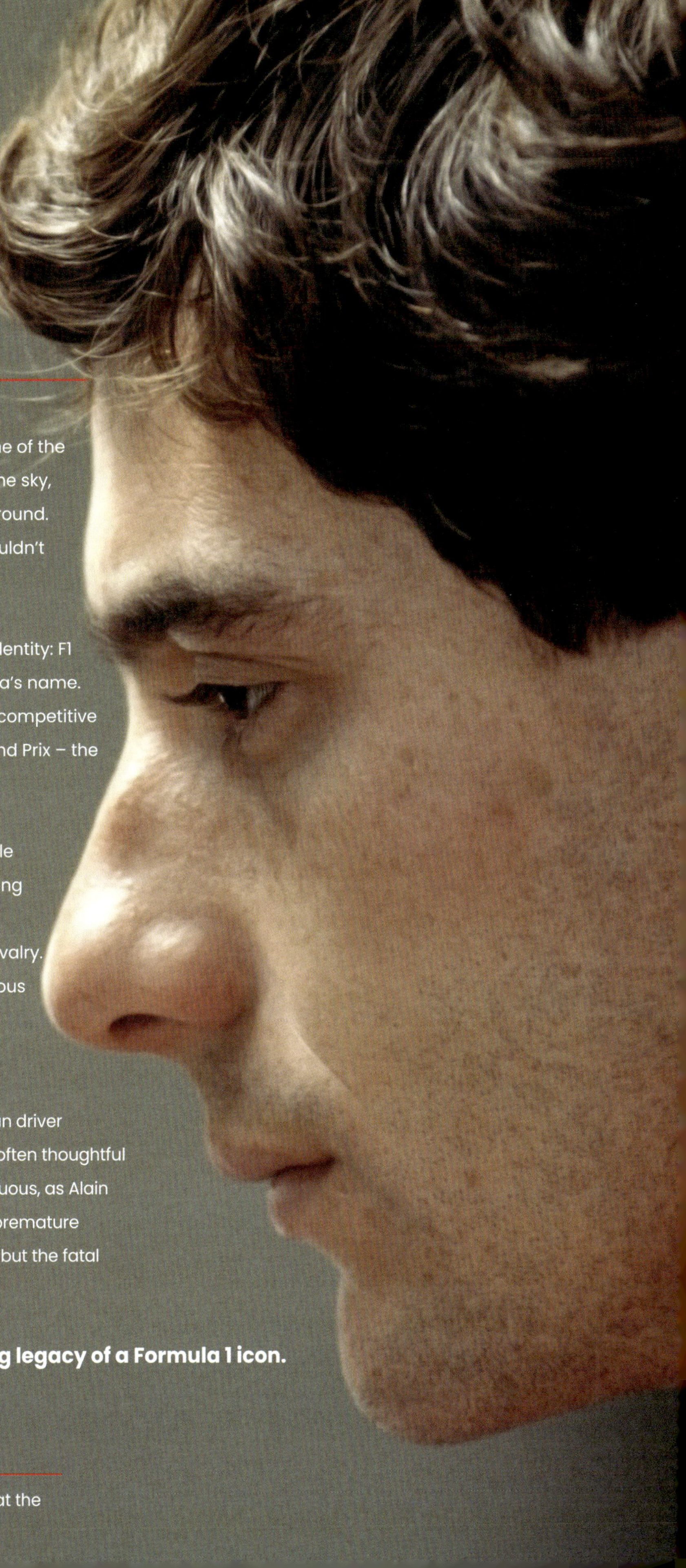

carrier bag. He put a stone in the bag and hung it on one of the helicopter's skids before sending it zooming back into the sky, trying to release the bag and catch it before it hit the ground. Even though the guest didn't quite manage it, Potter couldn't fail to be impressed with his ability and quick reactions.

Only after his guest left did Potter discover his guest's identity: F1 rookie Ayrton Senna. Before long, everybody knew Senna's name. Later that weekend, he drove his unfashionable and uncompetitive Toleman to an astounding third place in the British Grand Prix – the first of 80 podium finishes.

Senna's life came to an end 11 years later in a crash while competing in the San Marino Grand Prix. In the intervening years, he became a Triple World Champion. He broke numerous records. He was part of Formula 1's biggest rivalry. His yellow helmet became an icon of Formula 1, as famous as the livery of the cars that shot past at more than 150 miles per hour.

As Alan Potter's interaction with Senna proved, the Brazilian driver had a natural talent to control vehicles at speed. He was often thoughtful and introspective, but he could also be fiery and tempestuous, as Alain Prost and Michael Schumacher would later discover. His premature death robbed motorsport of a genius behind the wheel – but the fatal crash also added to the legend of Senna.

In this book, we'll explore the fast life and long legacy of a Formula 1 icon.

Ayrton Senna during pre-season testing in February 1990 at the Autodromo Enzo e Dino Ferrari in Imola, San Marino

EARLY LIFE

C1

Ayrton Senna's journey to the F1 World Championship began in a homemade one-horsepower kart. In his first years on the racetrack, Senna learned the fine margins and control needed to drive faster than his rivals. He also had his first moments of failure in his quest for a world title – an experience that would teach him that champions require a determined and ruthless edge.

Senna returned to his karting roots whenever he got the chance

It is often said that Ayrton Senna came from a wealthy family. It is also pointed out that such is the huge gulf between rich and poor in Sao Paulo, the most populous city on earth and Senna's birth-place, that wealth is relative.

But it's probably fair to say that when he was born, on 21 March 1960, his family circumstances were comfortable to say the least. Ayrton's father, Milton Guirado Theodoro da Silva, was a self-made man of humble origins. His first real employment was as a chauffeur but he later started his own business selling motor parts, which eventually employed 750 people. Milton also owned a drinks distribution business, together with 400,000 hectares of land in Sao Paulo state on which he raised cattle.

Milton da Silva was a down-to-earth man having strict moral values. He was proud to have made such a success of his business that he was able to support his family in a superior style compared with many other Brazilians. Indeed, Milton's wife, Neide Senna da Silva, was able to be a full-time wife and mother.

Ayrton was the second of the couple's three children; he had an older sister, Viviane and a younger brother, Leonardo. For the first four years of his life, Ayrton lived in a house owned by his grandfather, Joao Senna, situated on the corner of Avenida Aviador Guilherme and Avenida Gil Santos Dumont.

As a boy, Ayrton was highly athletic and excelled at sport, particularly gymnastics. Yet when he was three, he had suffered from motor co-ordination so poor he had difficulty climbing stairs. When he wanted an ice cream his mother had to buy two because one would inevitably be dropped. By the time he was four, Ayrton was developing an interest in cars and motor racing. Among his favourite toys was a Jeep which he pedalled around the garden. A few years later he was driving the real thing, changing gears without the clutch because he was too small to reach the pedals. His technique was to listen to the engine and change up or down when it sounded right.

At school he was a good if not outstanding student. Even though he was clearly intelligent and intuitive, Ayrton was not a natural scholar, having little patience with the constraints that school attempted to place around him. In any case, it was also clear that Ayrton was more interested in cars and motor sport. His physics teacher remembered him sitting at the back of the class drawing pictures of race cars. Ayrton was described as serious and having a maturity beyond his years but also as a boy who made few friends.

Milton shared his son's interest in motor racing. In the 1970s, Brazilian drivers were achieving success in F1. Emerson Fittipaldi had become the youngest world champion in 1972 with the spectacular black and gold Lotus 72, taking the title again in 1974 with McLaren. Milton built Ayrton's first kart for him using a 1 hp lawn mower engine. But he also tried to use Ayrton's developing passion as an incentive for him to do better at school, using the well-known carrot and stick technique.

Ayrton responded by working out the degree of effort needed in the classroom to please his father while still being able to continue with his karting. By continually dismantling and reassembling his kart in an effort to improve its performance he was also learning about the technical side. For his tenth birthday Milton bought his son a 100 cc Parilla-engined Kart but as he wasn't old enough to start racing officially, Ayrton had to continue practicing and developing his natural ability at home and on private tracks in Sao Paulo.

As soon as he reached 13, the minimum age to go kart racing in Brazil, Ayrton started at his local track of

Interlagos. For his first race there on 31 July 1973 Ayrton started from pole, a position determined by ballot. He took full advantage of it by leading for much of the race before colliding with a rival.

Behind the wheel his persona changed: he was focused, alert, attentive and fully co-ordinated. Many of the qualities that would later characterise Ayrton Senna on the F1 stage were now beginning to be displayed in the rough and tumble environment of karting. He was meticulous in his preparation and on the track he seemed fearless. He was unwilling to give way to other competitors even though he expected them to give way to him. He was also displaying a precocious and prodigious talent.

To help develop it further, and also to gain an advantage in this close and highly competitive arena, Milton engaged the services of a Spanish-born engineer who had emigrated to Brazil a quarter of a century earlier. Lucio Pascal Gascon, also known as Tche, was well-known as a tuner of kart engines and had previously worked with Fittipaldi and also Carlos Pace, another Brazilian driver currently doing well in F1.

Most of the Sao Paulo karting fraternity used Tche's workshop to fettle their engines so having the man himself build Ayrton's power units gave him a psychological advantage over his rivals. Among his competitors during these formative years were some of the drivers he would ultimately race against when they graduated to cars, including Maurzio Sandro Sala and Mauricio Guglemin.

Tche soon discovered that Senna's favourite race strategy was to go all-out to win. *"For him,"* he observed, *"the others don't exist."* But when he urged Ayrton to *"cool it"* and take things a bit easier, the boy had his own ideas. *"For me it's first place or nothing,"* Ayrton insisted.

Yet these tactics seemed to be paying off. Every year Senna moved up to a different and more advanced category and, moreover, with his father's encouragement. In 1976, he won the Sao Paulo title and finished third in the Brazilian championship. The following year he had his first taste of international competition when he went to Uruguay to contest the South American championships. He won.

That same year Ayrton graduated from the Collegio Rio Branco in his home town. He gained qualifications in physics, mathematics, chemistry and English. His grades were average; his karting success was providing a clear indication of where his real interest lay. In 1978, Ayrton won the Brazilian championships as well as the South American title for the second year running. But now he wanted to compete on a broader stage. That year's world championships were being held at Le Mans, France in September and Senna wanted to be there.

Through a mutual contact in Sao Paulo he was able to get in touch with Angelo Parilla who ran the DAP company, a leading manufacturer of karts and engines in Milan, Italy. In 1946, Angelo's father, Giovanni, had founded the Moto Parilla company to design and manufacture motorcycles and in 1959 he produced the first rotary valve two-stroke engine exclusively for karting. Parilla's engines were highly successful but Giovanni retired in 1968 and the company closed. Two years later, however, his sons, Angelo and Achille, founded DAP and in 1971 the company unveiled the Corsair engine which was to form the basis of the company's success in karting competition.

By the late 1970s, DAP was running its own team of professional drivers but was happy to take on others who could pay. According to Angelo Parilla, he and Milton agreed that Ayrton should go to Italy to drive for DAP *"for around $6,000 or $7,000."* That included *"equipment,* *mechanics, everything."* Milton also pointed out that his son was fussy about his diet and would only eat Brazilian food but when Ayrton arrived in Italy he quickly developed a taste for spaghetti.

The two conversed in a mixture of Italian, Portuguese, Spanish and gestures. But Parilla was sorry for the boy who had "*lived like a king*" at home in Brazil and was now staying at a small hotel in a country where he could hardly speak a word of the language. "*The first ten days were really hard for the boy,*" Parilla recalled.

But it was soon clear that the "*strange young man*" wanted to do most of his talking on the track. He wasn't interested in shopping in Milan or anything else, even getting to know the local girls. In August, the team went to the track at Parma, 100 km from Milan. It was a tight serpentine circuit with lots of corners. Parilla described it as "*difficult.*"

Even so, Senna was happy driving the kart there. It was all he wanted to do. He and the team spent three weeks at Parma where Ayrton encountered one of the stars of the DAP team. Terry Fullerton from West London was 13 years older than Ayrton and in 1973 had become the first Briton to win the Karting World Championship.

For almost a week, Fullerton tested between 30 and 40 engines before Senna ran them. When Angelo's brother Achille told the young Brazilian to go for it Ayrton did just that. After 10 laps he had equalled Fullerton's best time even though Ayrton had been using Bridgestone tyres which were softer than those he was accustomed to. This was sensational. "*What he did was astonishing,*" Angelo Parilla recalled.

At Le Mans, Senna had his first taste of international competition and was soon rubbing shoulders with drivers from other European countries as well as North and South America. The competition was much stiffer than anything he had previously encountered but that clearly didn't worry him. He soon gave notice of his intentions when he won the first of the three early heats. In the second he had scorched away from the start and disappeared into the distance. "*He was never challenged,*" reported the magazine Karting. He was forced out of the third with a seized engine.

In the three races which comprised the final, Senna finished seventh in the first and collided with another competitor in the second. In the third he came home sixth, which was also his overall position in the championship. At one stage he was challenging Lake Speed from Jackson, Mississippi who was to become that year's champion. For a newcomer to competition at this level Senna's performance was considered outstanding. Indeed, Karting called it "*sensational.*"

But Senna himself was dissatisfied with the outcome. It might have been the world championships but he had not gone there merely to take part: he was not used to being beaten. But he could take some comfort from the knowledge that he hadn't had the best tyres. Bridgestone refused to supply a set of its superior compound covers to DAP for Senna to use. Parilla did manage to buy some from another team, although they were past their best. Ayrton made good use of them but by the third final they were useless and he had to run on standard compound tyres.

Parilla's view was that with better tyres Senna could have come away from Le Mans as world champion. Perhaps more importantly, Senna now realised he was good enough to win the title. After Le Mans the team flew off to Japan to compete at Sugo but tyre problems kept Senna down in fourth place in the final race.

In 1979, he won the Brazilian championship again before

leaving for Italy to spend five months in Europe. His first competition was the Champions' Cup at Jesolo near Venice. Next to the world championships, which this year were being held at Estoril, Portugal, it was the most competitive meeting and represented ideal preparation.

From the first moment he went out on the track it was clear that Senna's technique was the same as before: to go all out to win. Irrespective of whether it was testing, practicing or racing he had to be fastest. His courage and ability were not in doubt and nor was his determination. Often, he was just trying too hard and he seemed unable to think tactically and hold off when it would have helped him.

In the final test session at Jesolo, he had a major crash when he lost control of his kart and hit an iron fence at around 50 mph. Although he wasn't badly hurt it seemed to take the edge off his performance. Parilla later explained that his engine had been transferred to another kart but that the mechanics had failed to notice the carburettor was damaged. In the final he was still trying too hard and crashed again but recovered to finish sixth.

At Estoril, Senna was among people who spoke his language. In the third semi-final, run on a purpose-built kart track which also used part of the grand prix circuit, he was lying second. He was racing wheel to wheel with his team mate Terry Fullerton when they crashed after the Londoner's engine seized. This was clearly one of those times when Senna would have gained more by hanging back. He only needed to finish second to take pole position for the first final but his desire to win at all costs had taken over. He eventually finished 11th and this was to have far-reaching consequences.

Senna and Fullerton were team mates from 1978 to 1980. Years later Senna startled an interviewer who asked him to name the driver who'd given him the most satisfaction to race against. Senna replied: *"Fullerton, Terry Fullerton."* The expected answer was probably Alain Prost but Senna explained: *"He was very experienced and I enjoyed very much driving with him because he was fast, he was consistent. He was, for me, a very complete driver. I have that as a very good memory."*

The interview, conducted in 1993 during the Australian Grand Prix at Adelaide, scene of Senna's final F1 victory, had remained hidden until its inclusion in the film Senna, made after his death. In 2011 Fullerton, the rival Senna never conquered, recalled: *"I was on the top of my game when Ayrton first turned up. I thought he was nothing special, really. You did notice this kid seemed a bit more intense than usual, a little bit introvert. There was a lot of intensity about him. And then when he went testing you saw a kid who was very fast, so you look at him in a different light at that stage and give him a bit more respect. He went on to prove he was very fast, a raw talent. That's exactly what he was."*

In making his comment about Fullerton, Senna might have had the 1979 Champions' Cup in mind. In the final Fullerton overtook Senna at the last corner to win the race. Afterwards Senna claimed he had been the moral winner and accused his team mate of playing dirty. *"I preferred to let him go even though the way he overtook me was against the rules,"* he insisted. Angelo Parilla preferred not to take sides. *"Terry Fullerton and Ayrton Senna da Silva are the two best drivers in the world. All the others are capable of good third places but nothing more."*

Even so, the 1979 World Championships came down to a contest with another of Senna's DAP team mates, Peter Koene of the Netherlands. There were three finals. In the first Senna led initially but finished fifth. In the second he worked his way up to second behind another driver from The Netherlands, Peter de Bruyn. But when the Dutchman's chain broke the Brazilian took the lead but lost it to Koene who went on to win.

In the third and final race Senna was victorious, much to the crowd's approval. Senna himself punched the air in delight, thinking he had won. Angelo Parilla recalled: *"I have many beautiful memories of Senna but of all the images the one that I will never forget is when Ayrton thought he had won the world championship in Estoril in 1980. I think there were something like 20,000 spectators cheering Ayrton Senna who had won the third final and was running around the track with a raised fist because he believed he had won the world championship."*

He hadn't. He had accumulated the same number of points as Koene and in the event of a tie the regulations stated that placings in the semi-finals would be taken into account. Senna's 11th place in the third semi-final following his collision with Fullerton counted against him and the Dutchman was declared the winner.

It was Parilla's job to tell Senna that he wasn't the champion after all and that he had finished second. Ayrton was inconsolable, sobbing at the back of the pits while Koene was receiving the congratulations of his team. Between them stood Angelo Parilla not knowing whether to laugh or cry in what was his team's greatest moment of triumph. Parilla recalled: *"The boy cried like I've never seen anybody cry in my life."* Senna was indeed upset. He had been beaten by a slim margin and he didn't like it. Cikfia, the international karting federation, sympathised. *"He will regret all his life not having been crowned karting world champion,"* it observed in its official account of the event.

Some consolation came with wins in the Brazilian and San Marino championships as well as runner-up positions in the South American title as well as the Swiss and Italian grands prix. Senna won the Brazilian championship for the third time in 1980 before leaving for Nivelles, Belgium for another crack at the world title.

After the opening heats Senna was lying ninth. He spun out of the first final but won the second. That meant that Senna, Fullerton, de Bruyn and three other drivers were in with a chance of taking the title. In fact, the Brazilian could be champion by finishing third, providing de Bruyn didn't win. It was a hard-fought race but at the end the Dutch driver was the winner, meaning that Senna was second. Again. *"Sylva had come close to getting the title,"* Karting reported, *"and was less than happy at coming second."*

Victory in the South American championships in Uruguay was scant consolation. The world title represented unfinished business and was to remain so. Despite the changes in his life Senna returned to contest the world karting championships on two further occasions but he failed to improve on the runner-up spots gained in 1979 and 1980.

By now Ayrton had reached a fork in the road. He wanted to be a racing driver but his father was keen on his joining the family business. Ayrton reluctantly enrolled in a business college in Sao Paulo where he studied business administration but he dropped out after three months. He had persuaded his father to back him financially for a full year of Formula Ford racing in Britain.

The next stage in the making of a legend was about to begin.

AYRTON SENNA'S KARTING RECORD

- **1974** Sao Paulo junior champion
- **1975** Sao Paulo champion; runner-up, Brazilian junior championship
- **1976** Third, Brazilian championships
- **1977** South American champion; runner-up, Brazilian championship and Sao Paulo championship
- **1978** Sixth place, world championship; Brazilian champion; runner-up Sao Paulo championship
- **1979** Runner-up, world championship; runner-up South American Championship; winner, Brazilian champion; San Marino Grand Prix; second, Italian and Swiss grands prix
- **1980** Runner-up, world championship; South American champion; Brazilian champion
- **1981** Fourth, world championship
- **1982** Fourteenth, world championship.

L: Ayrton Senna, at 3 years old **R:** Ayrton Senna driving a Kart during his childhood

THE FIRST RUNG

Twenty-one-year-old Ayrton Senna went international in 1981, moving thousands of miles from home to take part in the British entry-level Formula Ford series. Despite early successes, he nearly walked away from motorsport until a timely offer kept him racing single-seaters for another season. It was only at this stage that young Ayrton adopted the surname that the world knows him by today – before then, he was simply Ayrton da Silva.

C2

Senna's 1982 championship-winning Formula Ford car has been preserved for display

In the early 1980s Formula Ford 1600 was seen as the first rung on the ladder to success in F1. Several world champions including Emerson Fittipaldi and James Hunt cut their teeth on the nimble little single-seaters.

Even though they were powered by mildly-tuned 1600 cc Ford Cortina engines they were capable of up to 125 mph, much faster than 100 cc karts. Their power-to-weight ratio of 220 bhp per tonne with an 11-stone driver on board was not far off a Porsche 911's.

The cars had chassis constructed from welded steel tubes, relatively simple wishbone front suspension and a four-speed gearbox. No aerodynamic assistance was allowed and the cars ran on treaded road tyres. The result was highly-responsive handling and relatively low grip, perfect for training aspiring professional drivers and enabling them to hone their skills.

One of Senna's closest FF rivals was Dave Coyne. He recalled that, *"the racing was hard."* He added: *"A 1600cc car was the most difficult of all to drive correctly and FF1600 was never a pleasure."* One former FF champion, Wil Arif explains: *"Formula Ford was so competitive that to get the best out of the cars you had to drive them in a certain way, which meant sliding through the corners to scrub off the speed and avoid wasting time on braking."*

As numerous Brazilian F1 hopefuls starting with Emerson Fittipaldi and Carlos Pace had shown, Britain might have a cold and soggy climate with dull unappetising food but it was the home of FF1600 with several closely-contested national championships. It was also where many of the cars were built and where some of the most successful teams were based.

One of these was Van Diemen run by Ralph Firman at Snetterton. In the second world war the Norfolk circuit had been the US Eighth Air Force bomber base of Snetterton Heath. On a chilly day in early March 1981 it was there that a shy young man from Brazil with a fresh face topped by a mop of brown hair presented himself. Ayrton was not alone: his decision to go racing had been complicated by the fact that he now had a wife, a beautiful girl called Lilian de Vasconcelos Souza who came from a prominent Brazilian family.

The newly-married couple left sunny Sao Paulo for cold and windy Norfolk in the middle of winter. They rented a bungalow near Snetterton. Several years of international karting competition had not brought the young man out of his shell. In 1994, motor racing journalist David Tremayne quoted team owner Denis Rushen as saying of Senna: *"He was so quiet. He was always the guy you found standing shyly in the kitchen at parties."*

Tremayne added: *"He remained thus for many years, although it was only a short time before his English improved to the point where he could no longer be duped into greeting fresh acquaintances with earthy Anglo-Saxon."*

Senna had been introduced to Firman in late 1980 by Chico Serra, a Brazilian who was already established in international motor racing, having won the 1979 British Formula 3 Championship and participated in 33 F1 races for the Arrows and Fittipaldi teams. Despite the Formula Ford car being considerably faster than the karts Senna had become accustomed to, he apparently found the Van Diemen a bit tame. He told freelance motor racing photographer Keith Sutton, who befriended him early in his car racing career, that he preferred the karts. He said that the comparatively low-powered race cars felt slower than the karts which he had enjoyed taking to their limits. He did not recapture the same excitement until he started in F1.

Even so, in pre-season testing, tucked into the cockpit of

the pencil slim yellow-topped Van Diemen RF81, he was soon displaying all the confidence and aggression he had shown in karts, handling the car with calm self-assurance. Despite his lack of English, Senna quickly developed a way of communicating technical feedback with the mechanics which amazed them and team boss Firman.

But his relationship with his two Van Diemen team mates, both South Americans, was mixed. Enrique Mansilla from Argentina and Mexican Alfonso Toledano both had more experience of car racing. Senna and Mansilla would clash but Toledano befriended the young Brazilian and helped him with advice.

For 1981, Senna decided to concentrate on just two of the major FF1600 championships, one sponsored by ferry operator Townsend-Thoresen and the other was promoted by the RAC. Senna's first-ever car race, however, was one sponsored by another ferry operator, P&O.

Perhaps 1 March 1981 should go down as an historic date in motor racing history because it marked the car racing debut of Ayrton Senna. At the time, however, the FF1600 event was just one in a typically active programme of seven at Brands Hatch, which included races for saloons, modified sports cars and FF2000. Coyne dived into the lead at the tricky, off-camber Paddock Hill Bend but at the flag it was Mansilla in front. Coyne had dropped to third. Toledano, who put up the fastest lap was fourth, ahead of Senna.

The young Brazilian had pushed hard for all 12 laps and it was no disgrace for him to finish just 8 sec behind Mansilla. It was an impressive debut. Autosport magazine noted: "*Undoubtedly, we shall hear more of this young man.*" A week later the Van Diemen team was at Thruxton to contest the first round of the Townsend-Thoresen championship. This time Senna finished third after what Autosport called a "*thrilling, all-angles tussle*" with Mansilla.

Brands Hatch on 15 March was the scene of Ayrton Senna's first car racing victory. On his second visit to the sinuous Kent track he seemed to have absorbed its twists and turns because he surprised many with his speed at the wheel of the latest Van Diemen. There were two heats and a final. In the second, the track was streaming after a downpour but Senna's sensitivity and car control were such that the waterlogged track seemed to make little difference to his ability to hold off a determined Mansilla. By now Firman had realised that Senna was the best of the team's drivers despite the superior experience of Mansilla and Toledano.

There was another downpour at the start of the 15-lap final but after resisting early pressure Senna won by over 10 seconds from team mate Toledano. As her husband took the flag, Liliane was close to tears, knowing how much victory meant to him. He started from pole position for the third round of the Townsend-Thoresen round at Mallory Park on 22 March but Mansilla shot into the lead, leaving Senna battling with three other rivals. He eventually broke away from this group and closed on his team mate. He tried hard to pass Mansilla, finding himself on the grass several times.

Going into the final lap Senna emerged from the long loop of Gerard's Bend faster than Mansilla, enabling him to draw level. But according to the Motoring News report he was "*unceremoniously edged off on to the grass by the Argentinian and angrily had to settle for second place with Toledano right on his tail.*" The front of the Van Diemen suffered body damage. Senna was so angry that after the race he confronted Mansilla. Photographs show a furious Senna with his hands around the Argentinian's throat and having to be retrained by his mechanic Malcolm "*Puddy*" Pullen.

In the next two races, at Mallory and Snetterton, Senna again had to settle for second place behind the more experienced Rick Morris who was emerging as his greatest rival. But a win in the first round of the RAC championship at Oulton Park started some observers comparing Senna with Nelson Piquet, then on his way to the first of his first three F1 world championships. Autosport thought him a *"future world champion."*

Two more dominant victories over Morris, at Mallory Park and Snetterton, followed. Silverstone on 21 June produced an intense battle between the two and another display of anger from the Brazilian. Senna took the lead from the start but Morris reeled him in and passed only to be repassed almost immediately afterwards. The two were still nose to tail on the final lap, flat out at 125 mph, with Senna just ahead. Morris made a desperate lunge at the chicane which put him ahead. Senna couldn't contain his disappointment at losing to a man he considered to have jumped the chicane.

Two more wins followed but at Brands Hatch for the fourth round of the RAC title Senna found difficulty in setting his car up. He started from the third row of the grid but shot away from the start to dispute the lead with Mansilla by the time they reached Paddock Bend. The two were nose to tail going into the Druids hairpin where Senna took the lead. *"Such elegant car control can only be natural talent,"* enthused Autosport's Marcus Pye. Senna was able to build up a lead but with three laps remaining he had to come into the pits to have a water pipe replaced. He recovered to finish fourth.

Senna scored two more wins in the RAC and Townsend-Thoresen championships on successive days at the end of July. And there were two more going into August. By now only the three Van Diemen teamsters and Rick Morris were in contention for the T-T title. On a drying track at Snetterton the four were at it right from the start. But the rain returned at half-distance and, although several runners went off, Senna was able to build up a lead over Mansilla which he held to the end. That victory clinched the RAC title for Senna.

Among the spectators impressed by this display of car control in difficult track conditions was Dennis Rushen whose Rushen Green Racing team, was busy contesting the Pace British Formula Ford 2000 Championship, was effectively the Van Diemen works team. FF2000 represented the next step up from FF1600. The craggy Rushen decided he wanted the talented Brazilian newcomer in his car in 1982 and approached him to make an offer.

A week later, Senna's RF81 was a late entry for the Townsend-Thoresen Euroseries FF1600 round at Donnington Park. He won, challenged only by Rick Morris. Autosport observed that Senna *"really is in a class of his own in FF1600 this season and his fellow competitors must have been dismayed when his Van Diemen appeared as an additional entry..."*

By the end of August he had secured his second title, the Townsend-Thoresen championship. He took pole for the 11th round at Thruxton and took the lead at the start from Toledano and Morris. By the end of the third lap it was virtually all over; Senna was in complete command. This time Autosport's Marcus Pye was a competitor and got a close view of Senna's *"inch-perfect car control and absolute consistency."* There was still another round of the championship still to be run but Senna couldn't be beaten. He had 205 points to Morris' 136.

As it happened, Morris was victorious in round 12 at Brands Hatch on 29 September. Senna may only have finished second in the 20th car race of his career but under the circumstances that was certainly no disgrace. As the result of two first-lap incidents, when he clipped Morris' car and spun down the field before being hit by a back marker, Senna found himself at the tail of the field. His comeback drive was *"incredible,"* according to Motoring News. At the flag he'd climbed back to finish second and in the process set fastest lap by nearly 2 sec. That left him with 222 championship points to Morris' 156.

It had been a stunning debut season: out of 20 races he had won 12 and finished second five times. He had comfortably won both the championships he'd contested but instead of the immediate advancement he sought, Senna's success brought confusion.

At Brands Hatch on 29 September after clinching the Townsend-Thoresen championship he made a surprise announcement at the very moment of his triumph. On the podium, in response to a question from the race commentator who asked if was looking forward to moving up to Formula 3 in `82, Senna said he'd finished with motor racing and was going back to Brazil. His intention was to go home and work for his father. It seems likely that a key contributory factor in this decision was the attitude of his wife.

Lilian had found it difficult to adapt to her husband's racing life in England. Back in Brazil the couple decided to divorce. Senna never spoke about it but Lilian said: *"I was his second passion. His first passion was racing... There was nothing more important in the world for him, not family, not wife, nothing."* The marriage was dissolved in 1982. Lilian later re-married and had two children.

Milton da Silva had said he would pay for a year's racing in Europe and that year had now finished. Accordingly, he urged his son to give up motor racing and join the family business. Deprived of parental support, the only way for Ayrton to continue his motor racing career in Europe was with commercial sponsorship. But despite the success Senna had achieved none was forthcoming.

In fact, his achievements in Europe came at a time when other Brazilians were doing well in the international arena. Roberto Moreno and Raul Boesel were both winning in Formula 3, while Nelson Piquet was well on the way to becoming Brazil's second F1 world champion. But the Brazilian economy was not doing well at the time and there was high inflation which would lead to political upheaval in 1985.

Ayrton Senna was thoroughly disillusioned by the lack of support. Bitterly, he observed: *"In racing talent is not important; a bad driver with money can get a good team, but a good driver with little money can only get a bad team."* For four months he managed a building supplies business for his father but it was clear he was desperately unhappy. Ralph Firman of Van Diemen had stayed in touch by telephone over the winter and encouraged Ayrton to accept Dennis Rushen's offer. Milton da Silva relented and agreed to provide some money. By February 1982 Ayrton was back in England ready to race. His closest friends were Mauricio Gugelmin and his wife Stella. *"She was like a mum to him,"* recalled Keith Sutton.

Formula Ford 2000 had started in 1975 and was based on the 2.0L Ford Pinto engine, built by Ford Europe, mounted in welded steel chassis similar to those of FF1600 cars. The biggest difference was that wings and slick tyres were permitted to allow a level of sophistication and flexibility not possible with the smaller cars. Wil Arif who drove in FF2000 with Martin Brundle, who was to be Senna's toughest competitor in F3, recalls the cars as easier to drive than the FF1600s. *"They had wings and you could use slick tyres so there was more flexibility than with FF1600s and you could drive them more smoothly."*

Rushen Green Racing, based at Donnington Park in Derbyshire, provided Senna with the latest Van Diemen RF82. The team mechanics nicknamed him Harry. It was decided that he would contest both the Pace Petroleum and European 2000 championships. His main rivals would be Calvin Fish and his own team mate Kenny Andrews.

Because of the uncertainty that had surrounded the continuation of Senna's racing career, his return to Britain hadn't allowed him much time to become acquainted with the new car. It didn't seem to matter. He achieved pole position for the first race of 1982 at Brands Hatch lapping over a second faster than his rivals. From the start, according to Motoring News, he *"simply rushed off into the distance."* At the chequered flag he was nearly 10 sec ahead of Fish.

The next race, at Oulton Park on 27 March was pretty much a repeat performance and he continued his winning ways over the following four races. But in the first round of the European Championship, also Senna's first car race outside Britain, he posted his first retirement. It had been expected that at Zolder in Belgium, Senna would face stiff competition from the Dutch driver Cor Euser, the reigning European, Dutch and Benelux FF1600 champion. Senna had previously encountered Euser in kart racing.

Senna took pole position by a second and, although the start was delayed by oil on the track which caused his engine to overheat, he shot into the lead and pulled away from Euser. But on the third lap Senna sensed his engine was beginning to tighten and he opted to pull into the pits rather than cause more damage. Such mechanical sympathy was to become one of his hallmarks. Euser won.

Normal service was resumed at the beginning of May with successive victories on successive days. But in the second European championship round at Donnington Park, which he started from his by now customary pole position, Senna was troubled by a misfiring engine. He still won, though, and also broke his own lap record by just over a tenth of a second. The following day, at Mallory, however, he wasn't on pole but still managed to lead from the start leaving the rest of the pack scrapping in his wake. By now Senna had more than double the points in the British FF2000 championship than his closest challenger, Calvin Fish.

The following week-end the European title trail led the FF2000 runners to Zolder in Belgium for the third round. That same week-end the circuit was also hosting the Belgian Grand Prix and it was during the second qualifying session that the popular and much-admired Gilles Villeneuve was killed, casting a shadow over the rest of the meeting. Senna started the FF2000 race from pole and built up a 13 sec lead but threw it away with a spin into the catch fencing. Autosport called it a *"rare error."* Senna left Belgium second in the points standing.

The eighth round of the British championship at Oulton Park was not a success for Senna. It was, though, for Calvin Fish. Now Van Diemen mounted, he was on pole, won the race and set fastest lap. Senna was suffering from a down-on-power engine but encountered even more serious trouble early in the race when a rear tyre exploded at 125 mph at the tricky Cascades downhill left-hander. The car snapped sideways, but Senna demonstrated his exceptional car control by holding the subsequent lurid slides.

He won the next three rounds, at Brands Hatch and Mallory Park, but the fourth round of the European title, at Hockenheim, saw him post another retirement. Soon after the start Cor Euser made a misjudgement at the chicane which flung his car into a series of rolls. The rest of the field tried to avoid him but there was a major accident and the race was stopped. Senna's car was too badly damaged to take the re-start.

Things went better for Senna at Zandvoort for the fifth

round of the European championship. This was despite a clutch problem which caused him to miss the opening practice session on an unfamiliar circuit, although he took pole position. He made a slow start but once in the lead, he dominated the race despite gearbox problems, winning by just over 2 sec from Fish.

In between Hockenheim and Zandvoort, Senna won the 12th round of the British championship at Oulton Park but could only finish second at Snetterton for round 13. The track was wet at the start of the race, which Senna lead initially. But as the track dried he struggled to conserve his wet weather tyres and lost the lead on the final lap. He may have had to settle for second place, but he was still ahead of rival Fish in the championship.

As the season reached its climax so Senna hit his stride. From early July until the end of the season in mid-November he was beaten only once. He won ten races and started from pole position seven times. The tally included winning the last four rounds of the European Championship, at Hockenheim, the Osterreichring, Jyllandsring in Denmark and Mondello Park in Ireland. The Danish race was the penultimate round but ended up being the decider because Senna was so far ahead of Calvin Fish (43 points) that he could not be beaten. He finished the final race with a lead of over 20 sec over his closest pursuer.

The 15th round of the British championship at Snetterton provided a glimpse of things to come when Senna and Fish clashed on track. As they disputed the lead the Brazilian started weaving, edging his rival off the track. Fish's car bounced across the grass. He retired and subsequently lodged an official complaint. Senna's behaviour was criticised by the marshals and he was fined by the RAC yet was allowed to keep his championship points.

His only failure to win at this stage of the season came at Brands Hatch on 26 September for the final round of the British Championship. He had missed the previous round because of his determination to compete in the World Karting Championships in Sweden. However, his second place at the Kent track was enough to win him the title comfortably with 376 points to Calvin Fish's 271. He managed only 14th in the karting title chase which, it was thought, had put him in the wrong mood for Brands, although he failed by less than a second to catch Fish.

During the year Senna also competed in two car races which had no bearing on the outcome of either of the two FF2000 championships. At the end of May he took part in a celebrity race in a Talbot Sunbeam, which he won comfortably. More significantly, his final race of the season, and his 50th car race, was in a Formula 3 car at Snetterton. Since winning the two FF2000 titles, Senna had been back to Brazil *"to enjoy a little bit of the summer"* and to talk to sponsors about his plans for 1983.

It was clear which way he was planning to go. F3 was the logical next step and in June he'd attended a test day at Silverstone when he was accompanied by his father who'd travelled from Brazil to watch. Ayrton had been approached by F3 team owner Eddie Jordan – now an F1 TV commentator – who was looking for promising drivers for his new team.

Senna completed 38 laps and got down to a time of 58.03 sec on the Club Circuit. This compared with the best time of 54.4 recorded in the previous F3 race on the same circuit. Jordan and Ron Dennis of McLaren were both showing an interest in sponsoring the young Brazilian. But Senna reacted cautiously. He said he wanted to try other F3 cars before committing himself.

In late October he returned to Britain in time to test the F3 Ralt RT3-Toyota run by West Surrey Racing at Thruxton and Snetterton before driving it in the final F3 race of the year at the Norfolk circuit. The car (chassis number 291) had been used by Senna's former Van Diemen team mate Enrique Mansilla to claim the runner-up spot in that year's British F3 Championship.

"I went well in the car," was Senna's verdict. He also said he *enjoyed working with team principal Dick Bennetts."* They clearly took to one another. The West Surrey boss called Senna *"a very intelligent driver and he can tell me exactly what the car is doing, which makes my job a lot easier."*

Despite being televised by the BBC, the race was not particularly well-supported, many of the season's F3 frontrunners giving it a miss. However, Senna put the car on pole and led from the start. He made it look easy but afterwards insisted that he'd just been making sure that nothing went wrong and he that he didn't make any mistakes. He was, in any case, simply following his normal tactic. Afterwards, Autosport was in prophetic mood. *"Here"* the magazine observed in its race report,

"is a world champion in the making for sure."

STATISTICS

1981

Townsend-Thoresen Formula Ford 1600 championship 1st, 8 wins

RAC British Formula Ford 1600 championship 1st, 4 wins

1982

European Formula Ford 2000 championship 1st, 7 wins

Pace British Formula Ford 2000 championship 1st, 18 wins

Shell celebrities' race, Brands Hatch 1st

Non-championship F3 race, Thruxton 1st.

Ayrton Senna in his Formula Ford car in 1982

AMOCO
NDING NO AMPTON 0604 4734
RENISIMA
ERDE ESPECIAL
BANERJ

THE FORMULA 3 BATTLE

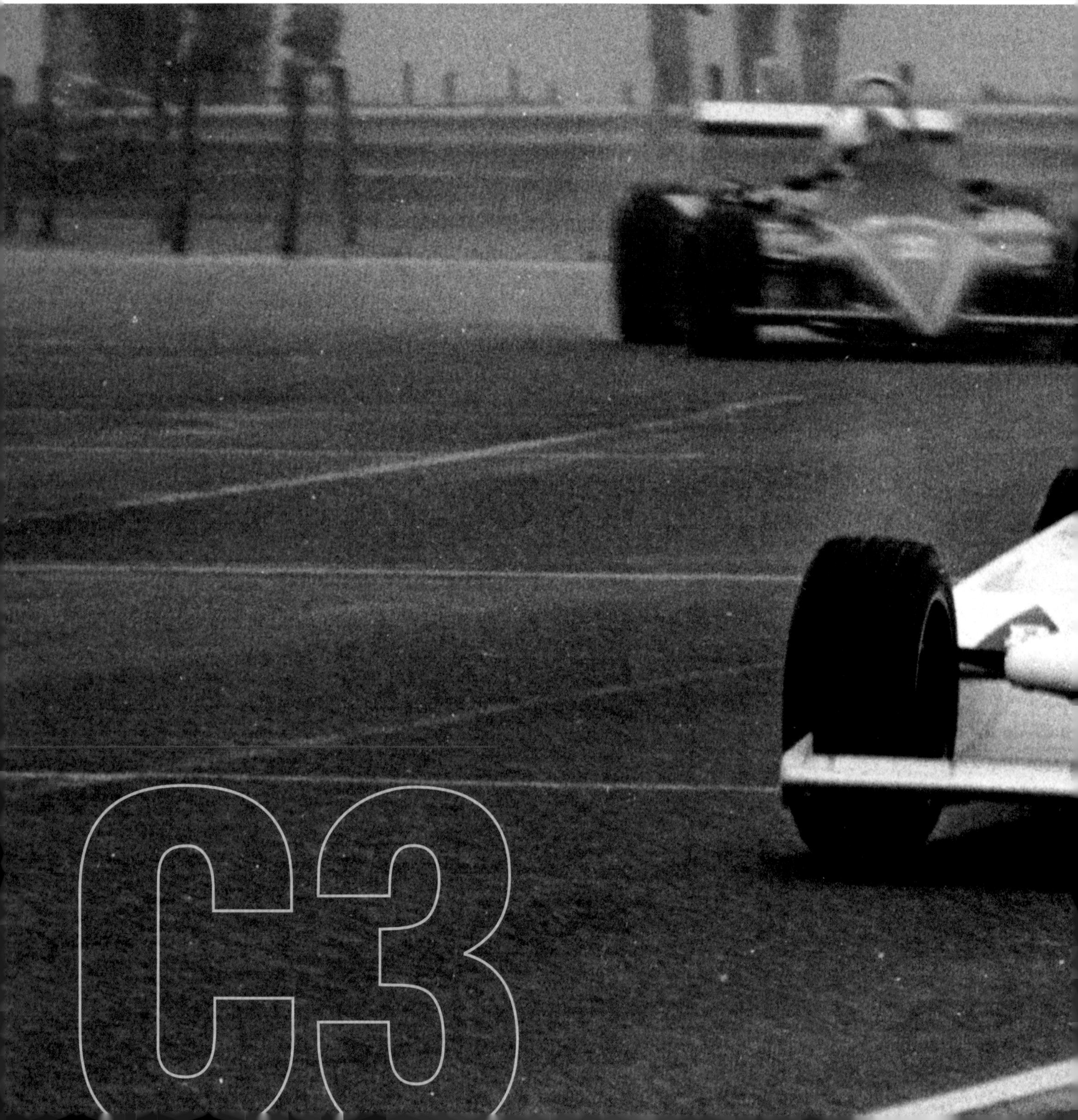

C3

After failing to take the World Karting title, Ayrton Senna found himself in another close-run fight during his single season in the British Formula 3 Championship. After dominating the first half of the season, Senna was forced to defend for the rest of the year as a rival took chunks out of his lead – and the title race went down to the final race.

Senna won 12 of 20 races in the 1983 British Formula 3 Championship

Martin Brundle's route to formula three was distinctly different to Ayrton Senna's, yet he was to become the toughest rival the Brazilian had yet encountered in his motor racing career. In fact, there was a point in 1983 when it seemed that Brundle might actually beat Senna to the title.

While the Brazilian was following the "*classic*" path from karts to Formula 1 via Formula Ford 1600 and FF2000, the King's Lynn motor trader's son had begun in grass track events, moved to short-track hot rods and then to touring cars. "*I was,*" he said later, "*just a hobby racer racing for fun.*"

In fact, Senna was still in karts in 1979 when Brundle was making his first steps in single seaters with FF2000. He stepped up to F3 in 1982 when he contested the British championship with the David Price Racing Team.

The following year the two men's paths would converge and the fresh-faced Brundle would become more of a threat to Senna's aspirations than the likes of Enrique Mansilla or Calvin Fish had ever been. With an F3 season to his credit, the Norfolk man was now being run by the ambitious Eddie Jordan whose overtures Senna had rejected. The Brazilian had decided to stick with West Surrey Racing with whom he'd won a non-championship F3 race in 1982.

West Surrey Racing had been founded in 1981 by a canny New Zealander called Dick Bennetts. He'd previously worked as a mechanic for Ron Dennis but when the Project Four organisation acquired McLaren, Bennetts decided to start his own team. West Surrey won the F3 title in its debut year with Jonathan Palmer and ran Senna's Van Diemen team mate Mansilla who failed to win the 1982 title by just two points. That impressed Senna. He reasoned that if the Argentinian, whom he didn't rate particularly highly, could do that well in one of its cars West Surrey must be good.

As the 1983 season progressed and the F3 championship came down to a battle between Senna and Brundle, their rivalry became highly personalised and the resulting needle match produced close racing. Huge crowds were drawn to the circuits with more watching on television.

What made the championship even more compelling for spectators was the way Senna built up a commanding advantage in the early stages, winning the first nine races in succession, only for a series of retirements to allow Brundle to close the gap. The Norfolk driver actually held the points lead going into the nail-biting series finale.

Most of the F3 contestants were using the latest Ralt RT3 ground-effects car, albeit with a variety of 2-litre engines, although both West Surrey and Eddie Jordan used Toyotas built by the Italian specialist Novamotor. In addition to Brundle, Senna was up against tough opponents like American Davy Jones, David Leslie, Johnny Dumphries as well as his FF2000 sparring partner Calvin Fish.

At the age of 30, David Leslie was probably the most experienced of these rivals. The Scot had already been an F3 contestant since 1981 and although he'd continue until 1984 he'd become better known as a touring car driver. He was killed when the private jet in which he was a passenger crashed on take-off at Biggin Hill.

Davy Jones would finish third in the 1983 F3 championship and was at one time seen as a serious American F1 hope. Johnny Dumphries, actually the Earl of Dumphries, would dominate the 1984 F3 title chase with Dave Price Racing and in 1986 would be Senna's team-mate in F1. None of them would be push-overs and it was no wonder that, even with his mountainous self-belief, the young Brazilian appeared more than usually tense when the 1983 F3 title chase began at Silverstone on 6 March. "*There's quite a lot of pressure on him,"* Bennetts acknowledged. After his first runs in the car Senna declared: *"I think there's more to come just through putting more miles on the car and improving the set-up."*

Leslie put his car on pole position after Senna spun on cold tyres in the first session. Despite being quickest in the second he still lined up second to Leslie but ahead of Brundle and Fish. It was close although Bennetts reckoned the handling balance on Senna's car wasn't quite right.

At the start Leslie and Senna were wheel-to wheel as they dived into Copse Corner but Senna drove around the outside of the Scot's Magnum 883 and into the lead. The Brazilian was aware he was pushing his luck. *"I knew I had to pass round the outside but I was worried about the grip on coldish tyres,"* he said later. *"I kept the power on and the car gripped."* It did indeed, and Senna grabbed a lead which he held to the flag. Brundle was second, just over 6 sec behind, with Jones third.

In the week before the next round of the championship Senna tested at Donnington Park and on the full Grand Prix circuit at Silverstone, but he was still not satisfied with the way the car was handling when the F3 runners assembled at Thruxton. *"Think it would be possible to make it much better with more time,"* he said. Of his rivals Brundle was closest in qualifying in the first, dry, session but still nearly half a second off the Brazilian's pace.

In the wet second session Brundle was faster but his time was still behind Senna's best. The rain had stopped by the time the race started. Senna made a perfect start and although Brundle tried hard to match him it was clear the Brazilian was faster through the corners. Senna realised he needed to look after his rubber because tyre conservation would be the key factor in the race. It was a delicate balance: Senna's engine was down on power so he needed to make up time through the corners. At the flag it was Senna ahead of Brundle by less than a second.

Ahead of the third round, Senna had a heavy testing accident at Snetterton but it didn't seem to have affect his performance in qualifying at Silverstone. Brundle was fastest for most of the wet first session but in the closing minutes Senna went faster still. This too would become a Senna trade-mark tactic: saving his best until his leading opponent had shot his bolt then post a time he can't match.

The rain returned, however, for the race and all the contestants chose to start on wet tyres. Senna took the lead at the start but went wide at Becketts allowing Brundle through. They were nose-to-tail down Hangar Straight but Brundle could only marvel at the way his opponent barged past on the outside at Stowe. When the rain came down heavily, a back-marker Senna was lapping almost collided with him and the race was red-flagged.

At the re-start Brundle jumped into an immediate lead but Senna out-braked him at Becketts despite putting two wheels on the grass. *"Incredible,"* was Brundle's verdict after the race. Senna hung on, holding the inside line for Chapel to lead down the Hangar Straight. By now it was very wet and Senna's wheels were throwing up so much spray that Brundle couldn't attempt to re-pass. The Brazilian kept the lead for the six remaining laps despite his fire extinguisher bottle exploding. When the times of the two parts of the race were combined Senna had beaten Brundle by nearly 2 sec. Calvin Fish was third.

Rain also affected the fourth round at Donnington Park. Senna's West Surrey team was able to put him on a set of new Avon wets and this gave him an advantage in the first qualifying session. But in the dry afternoon session Brundle was able to match Senna for the first ten minutes but eventually had to give in to the Brazilian. The rain held off for the race and the two leading runners were side-by-side going into Redgrave from the start. Senna emerged in

BANERJ
BUY BRAZILIAN GOODS

front and stayed there to the end. Brundle was hampered by a sickly gearbox. He had to hold the lever to stop fourth and fifth jumping out of gear. That meant he was nearly 6 sec behind Senna at the flag with Jones a similar distance behind him.

Despite a bout of flu, which was bad enough for Bennetts to wonder about allowing Senna to race, the Brazilian put his car on pole. He did admit, though, that he wasn't sure if he was going as well as he should be. Indeed, at the start he missed second gear and found himself behind Jones and Brundle, although he quickly dived past the Norfolk man at Campbell. He overcame Brundle's attempt at re-passing and passed Jones on the third lap. The result was a fifth win in five races for Senna with Brundle second.

In the three-week break to the sixth round at Silverstone, Senna went back home for a holiday, returning refreshed as he demonstrated by taking pole position, beating his own lap record in both qualifying sessions. Although Brundle led from the start, he missed a gear and dropped back to the midfield. Senna was left in command, using what Motor Sport described as *"his by now famous technique of pacing a race from his mirrors."* The magazine described his progress hitherto as *"truly outstanding, the Brazilian coping with intense pressure from one or two rivals on the odd occasion..."*

There were two more wins from pole position at the next two rounds, run at Thruxton and Brands Hatch. In Hampshire, he was challenged briefly by Brundle but was 3.4 sec ahead at the flag. At the Kent circuit the main talking point was Senna's speed through Paddock Hill Bend in qualifying on his way to yet another pole. Senna admitted to being *"right on the limit"* through the corner. Autosport noticed that on one occasion he had missed a gear, leaving his car without positive drive, although *"even that presented only a minor problem."* There had merely been a brief slide before the car was back under control.

«

Ayrton Senna during the Formula Three race 13 at Silverstone Circuit in Northamptonshire, England, 1983

The start of the race was delayed by heavy rain and when the cars came out to form up on the grid it was noticeable how Senna's car was surrounded by Brazilian media people and a large number of friends. They were not to be disappointed. He took the lead into Paddock and quickly opened up a gap to his pursuers who seemed to be in a different race. At the flag he was nearly 2.5 sec ahead of Brundle.

The ninth round at Silverstone produced Senna's ninth win – from pole – and made it look as though the outcome of the championship was a foregone conclusion. But the bubble was about to burst. On 12 June, Silverstone hosted the tenth round of the British championship which was also round 6 of the European title chase. This exposed the Brits to continental opposition but more significantly it meant a choice of tyres.

British championship runners were obliged to use Avon tyres, while the European contenders ran on Yokohama rubber. Although the Brits could opt for the Japanese tyres for this race it would restrict their eligibility for the European title. Both Eddie Jordan and West Surrey opted for the Yokohamas which put Bennetts' team out of its comfort zone because its track data was based on use of the Avons. It had also had no chance to test on the stickier Yokohamas.

This gave Brundle the chance he had been waiting for and which he had almost despaired of getting. He made the most of it, putting his Ralt on pole and leading from the start. He never put a foot wrong on his way to his first win of the season and that, according to Motor Sport, *"was more than could be said of Senna."*

The young Brazilian had opted to use tyres of three different compounds, against the advice of the Yokohama technicians and soon found his car suffering from oversteer. *"There was just no grip,"* he said later. Writing in Autocourse, David Tremayne observed that it was Senna who "*cracked under pressure.*" *He reported*: "With graining tyres he simply tried too hard, spun at Club and repeated the manoeuvre terminally at Woodcote in full view of a press corps that had come to respect his talent enormously but only barely tolerate his accusations that others weren't playing fair on the occasions on which Ayrton's temperament got the better of him." *Motor Sport noted that until that point in the season Senna had made just one mistake throughout the season.*"

But Eddie Jordan said: "*We broke Senna that once at Silverstone. We were beaten nine times in a row but we were all determined we were going to beat him.*" Brundle needed to have his confidence bolstered and the team kept telling him that he was as good as Senna. "*It became personal,*" Eddie Jordan added. In contrast to his Brazilian opponent, Brundle had made the right tyre choice at Silverstone. He'd also taken a risk by putting on more wing. "*All of a sudden,*" Brundle reported, "*I was in charge. Once I got in front I was going to do a Senna...*"

It was at this point in the season that Motor Sport and others wondered if the Silverstone result might have signalled the end of Senna's domination of British F3. That possibility added interest to an already riveting F3 season and this swelled the size of the crowd attending the next round, held at Cadwell Park. But if they were expecting a renewal of the Senna v Brundle duel they were to be disappointed. True, the pair were at it hammer and tongs in the first qualifying session but Senna made a rare mistake and went on the grass exiting a corner. He kept his foot hard down but ran out of road and slammed into a marshals' post; the car was wrecked and one of the marshals required medical treatment. Senna had to sit the race out and watch Brundle win from Fish and Jones. "*How he [Senna] failed to break any bones in the accident at Cadwell Park I will never know,*" Brundle wrote later.

Indeed, Senna also failed to finish the following round at Snetterton. He had to start from the second row of the grid with a car that wasn't performing as it should. Brundle was on pole and stayed ahead to win but not without resisting a challenge from Senna. The Brazilian had worked himself up to Brundle's gearbox by the 12th lap. Senna made his move going into the Esses on the penultimate lap. Brundle moved across to take the racing line but Senna's front wheel rode over one of the Norfolk man's rears and he was off into a high-speed spin. It was Senna's third successive failure to finish.

Senna blamed Brundle for causing the accident and called for an investigation of the accident. But this was Norfolk, Brundle's home county and Senna was left to contemplate his dwindling championship lead: 89 points to Brundle's 73. Bennetts reminded him that sometimes it was better to finish second. "*He found that extremely difficult to accept,*" the New Zealander observed, but added, "*he did realise his championship was slipping away.*"

Senna certainly seemed to have got the message by the time the teams assembled for round 13 at Silverstone in mid-July. He tested the car before the meeting and found it more consistent and was able to put it on pole following a set-up change. From the start Senna managed to eke out a lead over Brundle which he held to the flag. But a week later at Donnington he had to settle for second – for the first time in F3 – even though he started from pole. Brundle was in irresistible form and kept his nerve even though Senna was hard on his tail throughout the race.

There was more disappointment for the Brazilian at the next round, at Oulton Park. The meeting started badly for him when he crashed heavily in testing when a rear stub axle failed. The car needed extensive repairs and afterwards Senna pronounced it very difficult to drive. Brundle was on pole and the two main contenders were soon locked in battle with Senna clinging to the Norfolk driver's gearbox. On lap 28 Senna made his move, braked late for Cascades

»

Ayrton Senna after winning the Formula Three race 13 at Silverstone Circuit in Northamptonshire, England, 1983

BANERJ

Corner and attempted to dive inside his rival. The two cars collided and skittered off the circuit. Jordan protested; Senna was fined and his licence endorsed.

Rounds 16 and 17, at Silverstone and Oulton Park, brought a win apiece for the two championship contenders, Senna taking pole and the win in Northamptonshire but retiring at the Cheshire circuit. Pre-race testing with the car repaired after its accident reassured him that it was in good form. Although he was on pole at Oulton Park, Brundle took the lead from the start but Senna slid into the barrier at Druids and damaged his car too badly to continue.

He had a new car for round 18 at Thruxton but complained that it lacked balance. Even so, it was good enough to take pole position if not to take the win. Brundle jumped into the lead shadowed closely by Senna. At one point the cars were so close it looked as though there might be another collision. The pair traded the lead but then Senna slowed and headed for the pits with a blown head gasket. Senna's championship lead had shrunk to just three points.

The tension was rising as the pair met a fortnight later for the penultimate round at a damp Silverstone. Senna was in trouble early on, spinning off on his second qualifying lap and nudging the barrier. *"The car was OK but not really good,"* Senna reported. He started from the second row of the grid and caught Brundle who had taken an early lead. They stayed nose to tail for most of the race when Senna made a late lunge at Becketts. It wasn't on, but this time Senna decided to back off, play it safe and finish second. This handed the title lead to Brundle for the first time, albeit by a single point.

The fact was that Senna had won all nine of the first races but since the half-way point had won twice with two second places but posted one DNS and five DNFs. However his consistency meant Brundle would have to discard some of his points, meaning he had to win the final race, at Thruxton on 23 October.

During the intervening three weeks both leading teams worked hard to secure an advantage. Senna drove to Italy with his F3 engine in the boot of his car to have it rebuilt by Novamotor but denied Brundle's claim that it had been done under his supervision. Eddie Jordan claimed Ralt designer Ron Tauranac had produced a new car for Senna which incorporated aerodynamic refinements. All Dick Bennetts would say was that Brundle's Novamotor engine featured a performance-enhancing addition that Senna's did not.

But there was more to winning the title than having he best equipment. Bennetts had been worrying that Senna was not in the best frame of mind to go out and win the title. Accordingly, he approached Dennis Rushen and asked him to have a word with *"Harry"*. Whatever passed between Senna and his 1982 team boss, the young Brazilian responded by putting his car on pole. The final race proved to be something of an anti-climax. Watched by his parents Senna leapt into the lead and was never challenged.

But it was not as straight forward as it looked. To ensure his engine oil came quickly up to temperature in the chilly October atmosphere Senna had applied tape to the oil radiator which he had to remove during the race. He had practiced reaching behind to remove it but to do so he had to loosen his seat belts to give his right arm enough room. *"I was sliding around inside,"* he reported later. *"It was quite hairy."*

Perhaps it was fortunate for him that Brundle was also having his problems, struggling in third place with a down-on-power engine. Senna's lead over second-placed Davy Jones was now 7 sec and he was able to ease off to the flag. On the podium, accompanied by his mother and father, the new F3 champion paid tribute to his closest rival and told him he was the best British driver since Jim Clark. For his part, the disappointed Brundle realised the fight he had put up had given Senna's triumph additional credibility. *"We elevated each other into F1,"* he said.

»

Ayrton Senna during the Formula Three race 13 at Silverstone Circuit in Northamptonshire, England, 1983

BANERJ
ESTRELA
BANERJ
Jeans

Later Brundle would write: "*Throughout that 1983 season we fought each other hard but always within the limits. What impressed me at once was his professionalism and commitment. It was obvious from the first moment that he was something special. He seemed to know by instinct where the limit was – not after the corner but before it. His was a truly remarkable ability, full deserving of those three F1 world championships and more.*"

Autocourse's David Tremayne observed: "*Without doubt, Ayrton Senna is one of the most exciting drivers to appear on the scene for many years and his progress in F1 will be very closely monitored. Such driving talent is not seen every day and if Ayrton can only bring a little more calm to some of his decisions made on the track, few doubt he will develop into world championship material.*"

A month later, Senna was in Macau for one of the most prestigious races on the F3 calendar. As he had recently tested for the Brabham F1 team in France, he arrived somewhat jet-lagged. In the first qualifying session he was running third fastest until he destroyed all four of his wheels in brushes with the barriers lining the tight street circuit. In the second session he bent a gear selector but the session was conveniently red-flagged, giving his team time to make repairs. When the session resumed it took three laps for Senna to

Ayrton Senna during the Formula Three race 13 at Silverstone Circuit in Northamptonshire, England, 1983

snatch pole position. His car was now wearing the red and white colours of Marlborough and sponsored by Theodore Racing.

The race was run in two parts, the aggregate time counting in the final results. Senna led both but in the first he was briefly led by F1 driver Roberto Guerro who was stunned at Senna's ability to sweep past him on cold tyres, something he'd been doing on a regular basis in British F3. He led the second heat from start to finish. To Dick Bennetts, Macau was one of the magical moments of his team's 1983 season.

Organised by Theodore Racing's Teddy Yip, the post-race party at the Lisboa Hotel went on until 3 am. Bennetts observed:

"You don't do that in England when you're racing."

STATISTICS

1983
Marlborough British Formula 3 Championship 1st
F3 Macau Grand prix 1st

Senna soon found his calling when he began testing in Formula 1 – here in a Toleman

Senna with Gordon Murray looking over data from an F3 test drive in 1983

THE F1 SENSATION

C4

The down-to-the-wire finish in the Formula 3 championship didn't just draw the attention of motorsport fans and journalists. Senna's exploits in Formula 3 drew the interest of several Formula 1 bosses including Frank Williams (Williams), Ron Dennis (McLaren), Bernie Ecclestone (Brabham) and Ted Toleman (Toleman). It soon became clear that Senna's time in Formula 3 was over. He was ready for the top rung of the racing ladder.

Toleman competed in Formula 1 for five years, but only Senna made the podium for the team

For the last ten laps Ayrton Senna had been catching Alain Prost hand over fist as rain continued to lash the circuit. By lap 31 the downpour had reached almost Biblical proportions and Prost was gesturing to officials to stop the race.

In only his fifth Formula 1 race Senna had chopped the deficit to Prost, the man who by common consent was the fastest of the current field, from 34 sec to just over 7 sec. On lap 32 the inevitable happened and Senna swept past Prost in a great shower of spray as they crossed the start-finish line.

Then the race was stopped. For a brief moment Senna thought he'd won. But in motor racing, when the red flag is shown to stop a race, the results are determined according to the positions a lap earlier.

Even so, the 1984 Monaco Grand Prix has passed into F1 legend. The decision by race director Jacky Ickx to stop the race when he did was highly controversial. It meant that Prost won with Senna second. At first the young Brazilian felt massively disappointed but he would come to accept that his status as the man many fans felt had been cheated of victory was the defining event of his first F1 season.

Ayrton Senna's first taste of F1 power had come the previous summer while he was still contesting the British F3 championship. It was hardly surprising that F1 teams should be interested in the young man whose progression through FF1600, FF2000 and F3 had seemed so rapid and so inevitable.

According to team owner Frank Williams, Senna had approached him for advice in handling the offers he'd been receiving. Williams responded by offering Senna a run in one of his cars *"if it would help him get the feel of the thing."* So it was that on 16 July 1983 Senna arrived at Donnington Park to drive a Williams FW09.

After nine laps Senna was lapping as fast as team test driver Jonathan Palmer. After 20 laps he was about a second quicker. Then he stopped to say he thought the engine was on the point of destruction. There were no immediate signs to confirm this but Williams was impressed. *"After the first few laps it was obvious that he had a lot of talent,"* Williams recalled. *"You could tell he was the real thing,"* he told Motor Sport. But with Keke Rosberg and Jacques Laffite under contract the team had no immediate vacancy.

Although negotiations with other F1 teams were to start in earnest in late 1983, Senna had actually been receiving overtures somewhat earlier. Back in 1982, while he was in FF2000, Toleman had offered to provide an F3 budget if he would sign an option with the team. During 1982 photographer Keith Sutton, who had befriended Senna soon after his arrival in Britain, had started promoting the young Brazilian driver by sending news releases to the F1 teams.

Whether or not this prompted McLaren to offer to fund Senna's F3 season isn't clear but Senna rejected the approach from Ron Dennis as well as Toleman's proposal because he wanted to keep his F1 options open. Even at that stage he had sufficient confidence in his ability to believe he would be in demand.

He wasn't wrong. By the end of the year he'd had test drives with McLaren, Toleman and Brabham. He was highly impressive in all of them but vacancies for 1984 were few and far between. McLaren had Niki Lauda and was about to recruit Alain Prost, while Brabham owner Bernard Ecclestone had been keen on signing Senna but lead driver, and current world champion Nelson Piquet, had vetoed it. In any case, team sponsor Parmalat wanted an Italian driver.

Lotus was also keen to hire the talented young Brazilian. Team principal Peter Warr was attempting to recapture some of the glory days of Lotus following the sudden death a year earlier of its charismatic and innovative founder, Colin Chapman. Gerard Ducarouge, who had joined from the French Ligier team, had overseen the construction of a neat and potentially effective car powered by a turbocharged – this was the height of F1's turbo era – Renault engine.

In October 1983, Warr invited Senna to Team Lotus' Norfolk headquarters. After a lengthy talk and a tour of the facilities, he offered Senna a contract to drive for the team in 1984 for $50,000 plus bonuses in line with points scored. *"To my surprise,"* Warr wrote later, *"he agreed straight away."* Warr pointed out that he would have to consult sponsors John Player and partners Renault and Elf but when he approached the British tobacco company, to his astonishment they vetoed the idea.

John Player was adamant that it wanted a British driver in the Lotus team. As a result, Nigel Mansell stayed for another year and there was no place for Ayrton Senna. *"With great regret,"* Warr wrote in Team Lotus: My View from the Pit Wall, *"I told Ayrton that things were not going to be possible the way we had planned, and saw him sign for Toleman."*

In fact, with lead driver Derek Warwick moving to Renault, only Toleman had a driver vacancy. Toleman was a team which had achieved success in F2 but had yet to win at the sport's highest level. The Toleman Group had been founded in 1926 to deliver Ford cars from the factory in Manchester to dealers around the country. It later followed the manufacturer to Dagenham and set up a new base at Brentwood, Essex. By the mid-1960s it had become one of the nation's leading car delivery companies and control had passed to Ted Toleman, grandson of the founder.

The bearded Toleman was a man with a taste for adventure and he sought it in power boat racing and motor sports. Following victory in the 1980 European F2 championship, Toleman moved up to F1 with a car penned by Rory Byrne, later to become recognised as one of the sport's most gifted designers, and powered by a turbocharged Hart four-cylinder engine. By 1983, although underfunded, Toleman had put up some promising performances and seemed to be on the verge of success.

Team principal Alex Hawkridge couldn't afford to hire one of the top stars so had short-listed Senna as well as Martin Brundle, the man he beat to the British F3 championship. Both were invited to try the car and, according to Alex Hawkridge, *"it wasn't an easy choice."* But on balance the team preferred Senna's approach. What stood out, race engineer Pat Symonds recalled, was *"his ability to understand."* Where most drivers used all of their concentration and mentality just to drive, Senna was using 80 per cent, leaving 20 per cent for analysis. *"In fact,"* Symonds told Autosport's Adam Cooper, *"maybe it was the other way around!"*

By all accounts, the negotiations with Senna were anything but easy. Toleman's 1984 car would not be ready in time for the start of the season so the team would have to continue using the `83 car, the TG183. The cars would also run on the unfashionable Pirelli tyres while the opposition would be on Goodyear or Michelin rubber.

This was the background against which negotiations opened between Toleman and Senna. According to author Christopher Hilton, the formal proceedings began with a series of clandestine meetings between Senna and the Toleman team's public relations executive Chris Witty in a lay-by off London's North Circular Road. The two talked in Senna's Alfasud and the process culminated in a draft contract being handed over.

But it was not until early December, when the possibility of a Brabham drive was finally ruled out, that Senna got down to detailed negotiations with Toleman. Brundle, meanwhile, had signed for Tyrrell. Senna and Hawkridge finally met in the latter's Brentwood office with an open line to the driver's legal advisers in Brazil. Senna insisted on going through the text line by line and he asked for many clauses to be translated so he could understand them fully. It was the small hours of the next morning before they were finished. *"It was the most painful process,"* Hawkridge told Adam Cooper. *"He was extremely anxious that he didn't sign something that he'd later regret. That's the kind of guy he was – he was very thorough and very astute."*

The deal was for three years. *"It wasn't super-generous,"* Hawkridge admitted. *"I think it was £100,000 for the first year, £200,000 for the second year, £300,000 for the third year."* What was to prove one of the contract's most crucial provisions, and the one that occupied the most time during the negotiations, was the release clause. If he wanted to be released, Senna was required to state any dissatisfaction with his situation. He also had to pay the team £100,000 before entering into negotiations with any other team.

Senna went back to Brazil for the winter but remained in constant touch with key team members to seek information from them. Engine designer Brian Hart was asked about the unit's main characteristics, while team manager Roger Silman found himself being told how to organise pre-season testing. Silman wasn't happy but he was in any case about to be replaced by Peter Gethin, the man, who as a BRM driver, had won the 1971 Italian Grand Prix which has gone down in F1 history as the fastest ever run.

In testing at Rio, Senna quickly proved to be quick in the car but was quick to point out the differences between the Toleman and the front running cars. He was

Ayrton Senna in his Toleman-Hart TG184, Grand Prix of Monaco, 3 June 1984

MAGIRUS
Segafredo
ZANETTI
Candy
MAGIRUS
Candy
19
MAGIRUS

consistently faster than his team-mate, the former world 350 cc motor cycle champion and an experienced F1 driver Johnny Cecotto.

Yet the more the Toleman team saw of Senna the more impressed they became. One of his mechanics, Barney Drew-Smythe, recalled to Christopher Hilton how small changes to the car that Senna asked made a big difference to his performance. He was also *"a nice chap."* Drew Smythe said: *"He'd come into the workshop and sit on the bench and chat with you."*

Hawkridge got to know Senna in other ways. *"Before a race he went into deep prayer. It didn't have to be in the motorhome. You'd see him wander off and he'd just sit down. He didn't kneel, he sat, clasped his hands and prayed."* He told Hilton: *"He was religious in a very spiritual sense. He thought there was a higher purpose and he was part of that."*

His home race, the Brazilian Grand Prix, was significant in marking Senna's F1 debut even thought it was, for him, a short race. He qualified on the eighth row of the grid, hampered by tyres which were consistently shedding chunks of rubber at speed. But he had already caught the eye of Motor Sport's grand prix reporter, Alan Henry who noted his *"aggressive positive lapping."* Senna gained four places on the opening lap but quickly fell back so that by the seventh lap he'd dropped to 16th place. He retired on lap 9 with terminal turbocharger problems. Cecotto's race lasted another ten laps before he, too, was out from the same cause. *"What are we going to do about it?"* Senna wanted to know after the race. The result was new and more reliable turbochargers.

The South African Grand Prix run on the fast Kyalami circuit came a fortnight after Brazil. Senna thought the car felt *"pretty good here."* His best time on the first day of practice was good enough for 14th on the grid but he predicted he could go seven-tenths quicker. The following day he did precisely that. His next prediction was that, barring mechanical trouble, he could finish in the points in the race.

Senna started from 11th on the grid but early in the race he hit debris on the track which damaged his car's nosecone and altered the handling. He decided against pitting for a new nosecone and in a race of high attrition he slogged on to finish sixth, three laps behind the winner to make his pre-race predication come true. Motor Sport's verdict was that he had *"driven competently,"* but 90 minutes of coping with the damaged car's wayward handling in the hot conditions had left him badly dehydrated.

"He was totally exhausted," recalled Barney Drew-Smythe. *"He couldn't physically get himself out of the car. He had to be lifted out."* Senna was taken to the medical centre where he was treated by F1's resident doctor, the eminent Prof Sid Watkins, who was later to become a close friend.

Toleman's designer, Rory Byrne, initially sceptical about Senna, was beginning to change his mind about the team's latest acquisition. *"His feedback was excellent,"* Byrne recalled. *"He had absolute commitment and determination but I think he hadn't appreciated at that stage how fit you needed to be."* Senna, of course, had already realised he needed to work on his physical fitness.

Before the next race, and the first of the European Grands Prix, at Zolder in Belgium, there was more testing to be done. Accordingly, the team completed around 500 km of running at Brands Hatch, Snetterton and Silverstone as well as at Zolder. The new TG184 was on the way with its revised aerodynamics and there was pressure from the sponsors – as well as from Senna – to run it in Belgium. This was resisted, much to Senna's frustration. This was deepened by an electrical malady which afflicted his

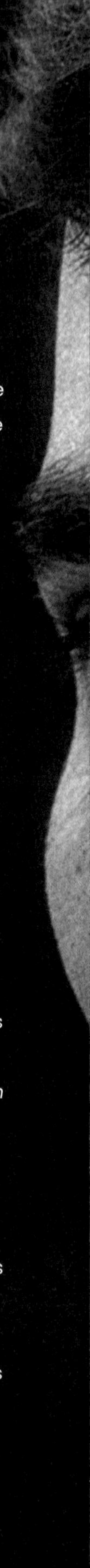

TG183B in practice and obliged him to use the spare car. The following day he was hampered by a misfire and ended up back on the tenth row of the grid. Another difficult afternoon seemed in prospect. A poor start didn't help but a steady climb through the field, plus a high attrition rate, brought seventh place at the flag, which was to become sixth on the disqualification of Bellof's Tyrrell - and win him another world championship point.

There were more problems at Imola for the San Marino Grand Prix. The tyre situation was becoming acute and the dispute between Toleman and Pirelli which had been simmering for most of the season so far began to boil over. Toleman had lost confidence in the Italian company and felt that it should have the opportunity to run on different tyres. Michelin was approached and after trying the car on the French company's rubber Senna was gleeful. *"It's a different ball game,"* he reported. *"Now we're with the front runners."* It was decided not to announce the change at Imola to avoid embarrassing

Ayrton Senna drives his Toleman TG184 Hart 415T finishing 3rd place British Grand Prix at Brands Hatch circuit in England, 1984

Pirelli on its home ground. Nevertheless, a fuel pressure problem prevented Senna from going fast enough to get on the grid and for the first and only time in his career he failed to qualify.

Before the next F1 race Senna was one of 20 drivers invited by Mercedes-Benz to take part in a race at the Nürburgring to launch its latest 190 saloon. Among the other competitors were past champions like Jack Brabham, Phil Hill, Denny Hulme and John Surtees together with more recent heroes Lauda, Prost, Hunt and Sheckter. If the organisers' intention had been just to lay on a bit of fun they'd failed to understand Senna's fierce determination to prove himself in such company. Accordingly, he finished the 12-lap race 1.4 sec ahead of Lauda with Carlos Reutemann third. *"Now I know I can do it,"* Senna confided to a friend.

Toleman decided to run the TG184 in the French

Grand Prix at Dijon. Running on Michelins – albeit older ones than McLaren's – the car should have flown but qualifying took place in the rain and no suitable wet tyres were available. Senna started 16th on the grid. At the start he made up a few places and reached ninth before his turbocharger failed. It was a retirement virtually unnoticed in the battle for the championship between McLaren teammates Lauda and Prost, but Senna would certainly make his mark in the next race.

At Monte Carlo the TG184 had a new engine management system which improved its response but did not increase power. Early in the first qualifying session Senna hit the barrier, forcing him to use the spare car. He eventually set 13th best time. Determined not to repeat his mistake, he spent much time learning the circuit.

Senna's performance in the soaking wet race that followed transformed him from an up and coming driver to one whose talent was obvious. In his race report Motor Sport's perceptive and much-respected "*DSJ*" – Denis Jenkinson – observed: "*If the race had been couple of laps longer Prost's brake-troubled McLaren would have been devoured by the fast-rising TG184 of Brazilian F1 graduate Ayrton Senna.*"

Later, Ayrton told his friend Angello Parilla why it had taken him so long to catch Prost. He explained that his engine had been delivering too much power for the wet conditions and that he had turned down the turbo boost. "*The more I turned it down the better the car drove,*" he said. By the end of the race he had "*no boost at all.*"

By the Canadian Grand Prix, two weeks after Monaco, Senna "*now appears to be on the shopping list of every team manager in the business,*" noted Autosport's grand prix editor Nigel Roebuck, another shrewd observer of the F1 scene. He thought that Senna appeared to be as quick through the corners as Prost and that he displayed the same "*fluent ease*" as the French driver. Nevertheless, he qualified ninth and finished seventh, two laps behind the winner.

The Detroit Grand was more fraught with a big practice accident on the first day. The damage was repaired and he was able to qualify seventh. A multiple crash at the start brought a swift halt to the race. Senna's car was damaged by an errant wheel and he had to switch to the spare for the re-start. Skimming a wall on this tight street service meant retirement on lap 20. At Dallas Senna clashed with team manager Gethin about the safety of the deteriorating track surface in qualifying. In the race he hit the wall several times before being side-lined by driveshaft failure.

There was another mid-season interlude when Senna accepted an invitation to drive a Joest Racing Porsche 956 in a World Sportscar Championship round at the Nürburgring. He shared the car with Stefan Johansson and Henri Pescarolo. Although they monopolised the car at first Senna was soon lapping quickly despite not having driven a closed racing car before. At the end of a race during which the team had a puncture, encountered clutch troubles and rainwater on the electrical system, the car was placed eighth. Senna, however, was not impressed. He told Angello Parilla that he didn't like sports cars and he never raced one again.

Of rather more significance to Senna's growing reputation was the British Grand Prix at Brands Hatch. Ten minutes into the first practice session Cecotto crashed heavily into the barriers at Westfield Bend, badly injuring his ankles. He had to be taken to hospital by helicopter. Senna was greatly upset by his team mate's accident but when the session was resumed after an hour's suspension, he was fastest of all including the two championship contenders, Lauda and Prost. In the first qualifying session he was fourth fastest, falling back to seventh in final session.

The race was run in two parts after proceedings were halted to retrieve a car stranded in a dangerous position. Senna spent much of the second part hounding the Lotus 95T of Elio de Angelis. Just two laps from the end he passed the Lotus *"on the run to Paddock Bend in classic style,"* reported Denis Jenkinson. That moved him to third place and his first podium position.

Looking back, Senna's Race engineer Pat Symonds told Autosport's Adam Cooper: *"I think Brands Hatch, when we were still a tyre spec behind was a fantastic result. To me that was more pleasing than Monaco."* Germany, Austria and Holland brought further retirements but events at the Dutch Grand Prix at Zandvoort effectively marked the end of the relationship between Ayrton Senna and the Toleman team.

Since his failure to get Senna's signature on a contract the previous year, Lotus principal Peter Warr had kept in touch with the Brazilian. Thanks to his performance with the Toleman, Senna had become a hot property and his market value had risen accordingly. He was still keen on joining Lotus and in early August 1984 – by which time, according to Warr, *"things had firmed up nicely"* – the two met at the Brands Hatch Hotel *"to finalise the details."*

The contract was signed later in the month. Senna's fee was agreed at $550,000, a little more than ten times what he would have settled for a year earlier. But Senna was becoming a skilled and ruthless negotiator and at a late stage tabled a demand for an additional $35,000. Warr reflected that the cost of buying himself out of his Toleman contract was £100,000 and although he wasn't clear why Senna wanted the additional cash he wasn't prepared to haggle.

The parties decided to announce the signing over the Dutch Grand Prix week-end with a news release embargoed for publication on the Monday after the race. It wasn't clear when in this timetable Senna was to inform his team, as required by his contract. And perhaps it was naïve of Lotus to expect an embargo on such a major news story to hold. It leaked and inevitably there was a big rumpus as Toleman took it badly. Alex Hawkridge was particularly indignant, accusing Lotus of acting in bad faith.

To add insult to injury, the Lotus news release contained the assurance that *"Senna will, of course, continue to drive for Toleman for the rest of the season..."* Toleman bitterly resented this patronising form of words, while Motor Sport's Denis Jenkinson, never one to mince words, made it clear where his sympathies lay. Senna, he said, had been badly advised. The affair came down to *"a simple case of bad manners and lack of discipline so prevalent in F1 since the advent of outside sponsorship and big business becoming involved."*

As a result the rest of Senna's 1984 F1 season proved something of an anti-climax. To punish Senna, Hawkridge banned him from taking part in the Italian Grand Prix. Warr called this *"childish"* but Hawkridge thought it the only form of punishment that would hurt. He was right. Senna told his Italian friend Angello Parilla that he hated F1 and everyone in it. Two weeks later Senna telephoned Hawkridge to assure him that he had fully intended to respect his contract with Toleman and that Lotus had jumped the gun.

The season's penultimate race, the European Grand Prix at the Nürburgring, brought another retirement. Senna started from the sixth row of the grid but his race lasted mere seconds as he was involved in a first-lap accident. The contest for the world championship between McLaren team mates Lauda and Prost overshadowed everything else at Estoril for the Portuguese Grand Prix and that included Senna's third place on the starting grid behind only Piquet and Prost. He drove a strong race to finish third and share the podium with Prost and Lauda.

He was the only non-world champion there.

At Estoril, Toleman at last had the same Michelin tyres as the other runners. "*We performed at a really high level,*" Pat Symonds recalled. "*It was a fabulous way to end the season with him [Senna]. We were devastated that he was going to Lotus and there had been that big fuss about it but these things usually get forgotten.*" Senna did eventually pay the release fee. Even Hawkridge eventually forgave him: "*I felt any racing driver worth his salt and given a better opportunity would take it. That's what he did.*"

In its review of the F1 season the authoritative publication Autocourse rated Ayrton Senna eighth in its top ten driver ranking, placing him between Derek Warwick, his Toleman predecessor and Nigel Mansell, whom he was about to succeed at Lotus. After what it called an "*unbelievable year,*" the publication said that the Brazilian's ability to step from F3 into turbocharged F1 "*and drive with such authority and speed merely conforms his opinion that he will be world champion one day.*" The only surprise was that he didn't actually win a grand prix.

Autocourse also noted that, "*His overwhelming self-belief is backed up by that natural flair and delicacy of touch which are the hallmarks of brilliance.*" But it added: "*He needs to learn that success may not come as quickly as he believes it should.*"

When Senna took his leave of the Toleman team, which had provided the first rung of his ladder to F1 stardom, he appeared to feel genuine regret at the parting. During the season he'd spent a lot of time at the factory finding out what was going on and talking to staff. On his final visit there he was seen to be weeping as he said goodbye.

Despite uncertainty about tyre supplies and deprived of its star driver Toleman continued in 1985 and actually achieved a pole position during the year but Ted Toleman decided to call it quits. He sold out to Benetton, the Italian clothing company, but stipulated that all the current team members should continue to be employed. Ten years later, the Benetton team, now with Michael Schumacher driving a car designed by Rory Byrne and engineered by Pat Symonds,

proved to be the main opposition to Ayrton Senna and his Williams-Renault.

F1 WORLD CHAMPIONSHIP STANDINGS 1984

Position	Driver	Points
1	**Niki Lauda**	72
2	**Alain Prost**	71.5
3	**Angelo de Angelis**	34
4	**Michele Alboreto**	30.5
5	**Nelson Piquet**	29
6	**Rene Arnoux**	27
7	**Derek Warwick**	23
8	**Keke Rosberg**	20.5
9	**Ayrton Senna**	**13**
9	**Nigel Mansell**	13
11	**Patrick Tambay**	11
12	**Teo Fabi**	9
13	**Riccardo Patrese**	8
14	**Thierry Boutsen**	5
14	**Jacques Laffite**	5
16	**Eddie Cheever**	3
16	**Andrea de Cesaris**	3
16	**Stefan Johansson**	3
20	**Jo Gartner**	2
21	**Piercarlo Ghinzani**	2
22	**Marc Surer**	1

»

Ayrton Senna at the Grand Prix of Austria, Zeltweg, 1984

Ayrto

Segafredo
MAGIRUS
MICHELIN
MICHELIN
19
SERGIO TACCHINI
SERGIO TACCHINI

Ayrton Senna & Niki Lauda after the Grand Prix of Great Britain, Brands Hatch, 1984. Ayrton Senna celebrating his first ever Formula One podium with winner Niki Lauda

Ayrton Senna in his Toleman-Hart TG184, Grand Prix of Detroit, 1984

Candy
Segafredo
Candy
MAGIRUS
Candy
SERGIO TACCHINI
19
Segafredo

Ayrton Senna in his Toleman-Hart TG184, Grand Prix of Canada, Circuit Gilles Villeneuve, 1984

Jacques Laffite & Ayrton Senna, Grand Prix of Monaco, 1984

Agip
SERGIO
TACCHINI

Senna's debut season saw him take on more established drivers like Ferrari's Michele Alboreto and Rene Arnoux

The wet Monaco Grand Prix was the highlight of Toleman's short stint in Formula 1

THE LOTUS YEARS

Given Senna's performances for Toleman, it was clear that he was too good for the team. By the time the 1984 season started, Senna was racing in the distinctive black livery of Lotus. The team was in transition after the recent death of founder Colin Chapman and Senna was a rejuvenating force, consistently outperforming teammates and returning Lotus to the top step of the podium.

Senna was the last Grand Prix winner with Lotus – the team folded after the 1994 season

One of the most iconic F1 images of the 1980s shows Ayrton Senna in his black and gold Lotus touring in after winning a very wet race with his seat belts undone and an arm raised. Waiting to greet him, arms outstretched and with a big grin on his face, is team principal Peter Warr.

If the Monte Carlo 1984 was the defining moment of Senna's first F1 season, winning the Portuguese Grand Prix race was the most significant event of his second year. Both races were run in heavy rain and showcased Senna's outstanding wet weather ability, but Portugal `85 was his first F1 win in only his second race for Lotus. It was the 90th car race of his career.

Three decades later in the summer of 2017, the magazine Autosport rated Senna's achievement as the second most outstanding wet weather drive of the modern F1 era. *"It was a mesmeric performance,"* recalled the magazine's respected former grand prix editor Nigel Roebuck.

Gerard Ducarouge's outstanding Lotus 97T and powerful Renault V6 turbocharged engine and Senna's obvious talent, his first F1 win had been just a matter of time. He was now partnering with the Italian driver Elio de Angelis, who in 1982 had won for Lotus the final grand prix of the Colin Chapman era and was well-liked by the team.

Since then Lotus, equipped with the Renault turbocharged engine, had been a front-running team but not a winning one. Nigel Mansell had left and now Senna was carrying the team's hopes of a return to the glory days of Jim Clark, Emerson Fittipaldi and Mario Andretti.

But to many observers, the current turbo era of cars able to muster upwards of 1,000bhp in qualifying trim and larger-than-life drivers capable of handling them would be seen as a golden age of F1 racing. Now Senna was about to become part of it but to make an impression he had to beat people like Niki Lauda and Alain Prost (McLaren-TAG), Nelson Piquet (Brabham-BMW) and Keke Rosberg and Nigel Mansell (Williams-Honda).

But first, the Brazilian new boy had to get to know his new team - and allow its members know him. His Toleman contract precluded testing for Lotus until 1 January but he arrived in Norfolk from Brazil suffering from a condition known as Bell's Palsy which paralysed one side of his face. This clearly called for another visit to Sid Watkins and although *"the Prof"* cured the condition, Peter Warr recalled that Senna *"was to retain a slightly lop-sided smile for the rest of his life."*

Warr and the rest of the Lotus team would soon come to understand the extent of the newcomer's contribution. *"His application to his work was all-consuming,"* Warr would write, *"his thirst for more and more expertise at his work unflagging. Always amazingly alert and aware and right at the nub of the current problem to be sorted, he would not let up until he felt he had given his best shot."* Gerard Ducarouge had been a Senna supporter since the previous year. *"It's not a question of if he will be world champion,"* he would say, *"but when."*

During testing at Rio before the Brazilian Grand Prix Senna clashed with Mansell – not for the last time, as it would turn out – and both cars were damaged. Later, he qualified fourth for the race itself, his first with his new team. He ran with the leaders but retired after 52 laps with problems variously described as engine electronics and suspension mountings. It was a very different story two weeks later at Estoril, a race which, it would be fair to say, Senna dominated. He was fastest in both qualifying sessions to achieve his first pole position.

The race was run in conditions which Senna described

as worse than Monaco `84. Warr believed *"most people would not take the dog for a walk"* in such rain. Senna led from the start and finished the first lap 2.7 sec ahead of his more experienced team mate, Elio de Angelis. By half distance his lead had increased to 37 sec. *"The big danger,"* Senna said after the race, *"was that conditions changed all the time. It was difficult to keep the car in a straight line sometimes and for sure the race should have been stopped."* Only nine of the 26 starters were classified as finishers and Senna lapped all bar the second man, Alboreto.

Afterwards, Motor Sport's Dennis Jenkinson congratulated Senna and said he was stunned by the way the Brazilian's lightning reactions in catching the car when, at one point, all four wheels were on the grass. Senna's response demonstrated what Peter Warr called his *"ruthless honesty with himself." "Rubbish,"* he snorted, *"that was pure luck. I was completely out of control and the car just came back."*

According to Autosport's Nigel Roebuck, *"just occasionally comes a race when one driver makes the rest look ordinary, and this was one such. He had been in a different class right from the green light."*

One of the secrets of Senna's wet weather ability was later revealed by his sister, Viviane. She explained that during his karting days he had lost a race in wet conditions. Feeling that he should have won, whenever it rained her brother would take his kart out for practice sessions.

Although Senna would be a factor in most of 1985's other races, looking a likely winner on several occasions, it was not until the Austrian Grand Prix, when he started 22nd due to engine problems in qualifying, that he again scored world championship points. Despite his engine continuing to lack power and vibration from his front tyres, Senna was able to haul himself up to second behind the winner, Prost.

His only other win came at Spa in September on the second attempt to run the Belgian Grand Prix following problems with a newly-relaid track surface. After a troubled qualifying Senna started second but jumped into an early lead in wet conditions. Initially he had to hold off the two Williams-Hondas, whose engines, Dennis Jenkinson observed, sounded *"very healthy indeed."* Senna's by contrast was starting to splutter occasionally *"and did not sound anything like so purposeful."* However, Senna hung on to win following a change to dry tyres as conditions improved. He finished nearly 20 sec ahead of Mansell. Later, Senna acknowledged, it had been a difficult race, *"because the track was never completely dry and particularly bad when there was rain in only one part."*

This victory not only conformed Senna's wet weather ability but also highlighted a problem that had been largely concealed from the public by Team Lotus and Renault. During the year Senna had posted seven retirements, prompting suggestions that he was abusing the machinery and overdoing his use of the turbo boost control. Yet the Lotus 97T had the best chassis of any car competing that season with the best braking and turning capabilities and the best designed suspension. Its Renault was known to be fuel inefficient under regulations limiting tank capacity to 220L.

Peter Warr revealed that constant adverse press comment nearly led to the end of the relationship between Lotus and Renault midway through 1985. Senna had already lost the San Marino Grand Prix when he ran out of fuel before the end – as did several other drivers – but matter came to a head when he was forced to pull out of the British Grand Prix, which he led from the start, with what appeared to be lack of fuel.

Warr later said that he had demanded that Renault, whose engine featured a number of *"secret"* performance-enhancing components, to come clean about the real cause of Senna's retirement. Team Lotus then issued a press release that one of these components, a gas temperature sensor in the left-hand exhaust, had failed. This disclosure revealed more details of Renault's electronic engine management system than the French company was willing to disclose and there was a big row.

"The truth was," Warr admitted, *"so many times that year we and Renault had let Ayrton down in his quest for what realistically was a genuine chance at the championship and any other course of action would have betrayed our driver's inherent and ruthless honesty."*

It was a similar story in 1986. Lotus produced the 98T, a developed version of the previous 97T. Elio de Angelis left to join Brabham, leaving a vacancy which Lotus and its sponsor wanted to fill with the British driver Derek Warwick, now free following the withdrawal of Renault's F1 team. Senna, however, made himself highly unpopular with British fans by vetoing Warwick's selection.

He argued that Team Lotus lacked the resources to run two leading drivers and feared that Warwick's inclusion would mean a dilution of the team's concentration on him. *"Senna was not frightened by the competition,"* insisted his biographer Christopher Hilton, *"never had been, never would, but he was frightened of the dissipation."* Senna threatened to walk out if Warwick joined the team and Lotus and John Player took him seriously. The result was that in 1986 he was partnered by Johnny Dumphries.

It was to have been the year things came together

Ayrton Senna in his Lotus-Renault 97T, Grand Prix of Monaco, 1985

John Player Speci
Ayrton Senna
John Player
elf
NACIONAL
2

for Senna. Renault had abandoned its own race team leaving Lotus as effectively its works team. Its new engine, the EF15, bristled with clever features such as the pneumatic valve spring system which allowed the unit to be lighter and smaller and to run even faster. Fuel tank capacity had been reduced to 195L, which Senna felt prevented him from really racing.

"Too many times," Peter Warr recalled, "did he have to drive with one eye on the fuel meter and see Piquet and Mansell in the Honda-engined Williams, or Prost and Rosberg in the McLaren-TAG's cruise by in the race. Too many times did he finish with dry tanks even though he was using minimum race boost. Waving his opponents through was not his style nor the way in which he wished to go racing."

As it was he achieved two wins and was on the podium eight times. He started from pole position in half the year's 16 races but there were six retirements as, once again, the Lotus 98T-Renault combination lacked the reliability to give Senna the shot at the championship his talent warranted. The year was dominated by the Williams-Hondas even though it was Alain Prost finally emerged victorious to secure back-to-back titles. Although Lotus finished third in the constructors' world championship, it's points tally was some way behind that of Williams and McLaren in the points standings.

In Brazil, Senna led from pole but had to give best to fellow countryman and rival Williams-Honda mounted Nelson Piquet but in Spain he narrowly beat Piquet's team mate Mansell to win by just 0.014 sec after the Englishman stopped to change tyres. This elevated Senna to the top of the championship table. He stayed there with third place in Monaco and second in Belgium but lost the lead with fifth place in Canada.

He was on pole for the US Grand Prix East on the tight street circuit of Detroit and he and Mansell tussled initially until the Williams was crippled by severe brake troubles. After a change of tyres, following a puncture, Senna regained the lead which he held to the end in a race which for once was not determined by fuel consumption. Senna's engineer Nigel Stepney was sure his man had plenty in hand. *"At Detroit and places like that he blasted off into the distance but he still wasn't pushing it any more than he had to."*

This put Senna back at the head of the championship table but not for long – there would be no further wins before the end of the season. Two retirements were followed by second places in Germany and Hungary and then two more DNFs, in Austria and Italy. Pole positions in Portugal and Mexico gained a fourth and third positions but the year ended with a further retirement – attributed to engine trouble – in Australia.

Much earlier in the season Senna had been looking for a way of improving his situation. At the Spanish Grand

Alain Prost of McLaren and Ayrton Senna of Lotus at 1986 Monaco Grand Prix

Turbo
RENAULT
John Player Special
elf
12

Prix, only the second of the season, he told Warr that he would only stay with Lotus for a third year if it had Honda engines. The Lotus team principal's response was to arrange a discrete meeting with Nobuhiko Kawamoto, Honda's head of research and development and the man in charge of the racing programme.

Clearly the meeting went well because Warr recalled that they ended up discussing the possibility of a Japanese driver joining the team to drive alongside Senna. The name of Satoru Nakajima, Honda's test driver was mentioned. Warr agreed and by Detroit the deal was done. Three weeks later Warr met Senna and his advisers in the Lotus motorhome at Brands Hatch to consider the Brazilian's contract for 1987. The outcome, according to Warr, was a two-year deal worth $2.6 million. Meanwhile, Renault had to be told that Lotus would be motivated by Honda power in `87. Warr recalled that he and Senna met the French manufacturer to explain why they wanted to change with the result was that Renault agreed to release Lotus from its agreement. The result was that Renault stopped supplying other customer teams.

At that time it was assumed that John Player would continue to sponsor Team Lotus but the tobacco company's new owners had other ideas and withdrew their support. To replace its title sponsor Team Lotus turned to the US tobacco company R J Reynolds which meant that the familiar black and gold livery Lotus F1 cars had worn for so long was replaced by the bright yellow and blue of the Camel brand of cigarettes.

This change enabled the astute Senna to claim that this change invalidated the previous deal with Lotus. The result was that his fee almost doubled to $5 million.

Meanwhile, Ducarouge was working on a revised version of the Lotus 98T to use Honda instead of Renault power. Senna might have got the Honda engines he craved that would enable him to compete with Piquet and Mansell but Honda's existing deal with Williams gave the Didcot team exclusive use of the 1987-specification RA167-E units. Lotus had to make do with 1986-spec RA166-E units.

The resulting power deficiency came in addition to the 5 per cent of power which would be diverted to drive the electronic active suspension system which Lotus planned to use in 1987. This system, with which the team had briefly experimented in 1983, offered consistent ride height with no pitch or roll in the chassis. The result, however, was a highly complex and heavier car. The mechanical components required by the suspension

system plus the engine-driven pump for the high-pressure hydraulics. It came, however, with significant weight and power penalties.

Ducarouge worked hard to find compensating aerodynamic improvements. Although Senna could see the advantages of the active system and refused from the start of the season to drive the passive car he considered the 99T to be little more than the previous year's 98T with a Honda engine. It was indeed considered to be one of the bulkiest of 1987's winning cars and to be inferior aerodynamically to its Williams, McLaren and Ferrari competitors. But in Senna's hands it was often among the fastest in a straight line.

The 99T was arguably the most advanced car F1 had yet seen and it helped move the sport into the digital age. But reliability problems dogged the 99T early in the `87 season and the system was a nightmare for chief mechanic Nigel Stepney and his crew. Yet Senna was determined that if active suspension would make the 99T go faster he would persist with it. In 2017 Peter Wright, the man charged with making it work, told Autosport's Adam Cooper that he believed Senna could see the system's potential even if he wasn't convinced it was that good.

Ayrton Senna in his Lotus-Honda 99T, Grand Prix of Belgium, Spa-Francorchamps, 1987

Neither he nor the team realised the affect active suspension would have on the tyres. At a Brands Hatch test day Senna reported that it took longer to get the tyres up to qualifying performance but that they retained their optimum performance for longer. Active ride made street races a lot less arduous but it took the edge off Senna's blinding speed in qualifying. Over the previous two years he had set 15 poles in 32 races, while in 1987 he took just one.

Despite the initial reliability problems the 99T allowed Senna to finish more races than he had in the previous two years. He retired from the Brazilian Grand Prix with oil pressure problems but the other two retirements, from the Belgian and Mexican grands prix were due to accidents.

In Belgium, for the third race of the year, Senna's Lotus and Mansell's Williams collided while disputing the same piece of track. Motor Sport blamed the Englishman for "*foolishly*" attempting to go round the outside of the Lotus on the tight Les Combes right-hander. Mexico, much later in the year, saw Senna's title hopes finally disappear. Towards the end of the race he was coping with the lack of a clutch when he locked his brakes and spun off.

Senna beckoned the marshals to give him a push. But when they failed to respond as he thought they should he jumped out of his car and, according to Autocourse, vented his fury on the unfortunate individual standing nearest to him." *The journal added*: "*It was also unfortunate that the television cameras were still focused on his little altercation.*" Senna was later fined $15,000 for striking a marshal.

More meritorious was his drive in the German Grand Prix at Hockenheim where the active suspension system's hydraulics failed. With no pressure in the system the chassis lowered itself on to the helper springs. "*At the highest top speed circuit in Europe,*" recalled Peter Warr, "*with the belly of the car dragging on the ground, he brought the car home in third place.*"

But the highlight of Senna's 1987 were his two victories, at Monte Carlo and Detroit, two street circuits. The Monaco Grand Prix was the first to be won by a car with active suspension, even though he had played second fiddle to Mansell in practice and in the opening stages of the race. But when the Williams-Honda retired on the 30th lap the Lotus river was handed the lead – and the victory – on a plate, although he reported having trouble with gear selection in the later stages. At the end of the 78-lap race Senna was 33 sec ahead of his fellow Brazilian and great rival Nelson Piquet.

Mansell was again the pace-setter at Detroit but Senna got the better of him to score his second successive win and elevate himself to the head of the championship table. Mansell had built up a substantial early lead but Senna dropped back with a soft brake pedal. Mansell stopped to change tyres, but easing off had enabled Senna to avoid a stop and he was again victorious from Piquet.

The final event of the year, the Australian Grand Prix at Adelaide, was also a street race and although he no longer had a chance at the title he was looking forward to it. Again avoiding a stop for new tyres he was able to finish second to Berger in the resurgent Ferrari. But another team protested the brake ducting on the Lotus and Senna was disqualified. He was furious, blaming the team for losing him second place in the world championship table.

It was a sad end to his three-year association with Lotus. But he had decided by mid- season to join McLaren and he walked out of the team's garage at Adelaide without a backward glance or even saying goodbye.

Despite the ups and downs of the season, Autocourse

»

Satoru Nakajima & Ayrton Senna, Grand Prix of Hungary, Hungaroring, 1987

CAMEL
GOODYEAR
MICROMAX
POWERED by
HONDA
DeLonghi
elf
Canon
EAGLE

F1 WORLD CHAMPIONSHIP STANDINGS 1985

Position	Driver	Points
1	Alain Prost	73
2	Michele Alboreto	53
3	Keke Rosberg	40
4	**Ayrton Senna**	**38**
5	Elio de Angelis	33
6	Nigel Mansell	31
7	Stefan Johansson	26
8	Nelson Piquet	21
9	Jacques Laffite	16
10	Niki Lauda	14
11	Thierry Boutsen	11
12	Patrick Tambay	11
13	Marc Surer	5
14	Derek Warwick	5
15	Philippe Streiff	4
16	Stephan Bellof	4
17	Ivan Capelli	3
18	Rene Arnoux	3
19	Andrea de Cesaris	3
20	Gerhard Berger	3

F1 WORLD CHAMPIONSHIP STANDINGS 1986

Position	Driver	Points
1	Alain Prost	72
2	Nigel Mansell	70
3	Nelson Piquet	69
4	**Ayrton Senna**	**55**
5	Stefan Johansson	23
6	Keke Rosberg	22
7	Gerhard Berger	17
8	Michele Alboreto	14
9	Rene Arnoux	14
10	Jacques Laffite	14
11	Martin Brundle	8
12	Alan Jones	4
13	Johnny Dumphries	3
14	Philippe Streiff	3
15	Teo Fabi	2
16	Riccardo Patrese	2
17	Patrick Tambay	2
18	Philippe Alliot	1
19	Chrsitian Danner	1

rated him the third best driver of the year behind Prost and Mansell, observing it was a pity that the Brazilian *"had allowed his emotions to get the better of him at Mexico."* The unpredictable behaviour in and out of an admittedly difficult car had tarnished an otherwise mature season of perseverance with the Lotus. The publication thought that his drive at Detroit was *"perhaps one of the best all-round drives by a race winner."*

Peter Warr believed that Senna and his special strengths had *"transformed the fortunes of Team Lotus."* It did not, however, work the other way. In three years, Senna had run 48 races with the team and won just six of them. Even with the Honda engine, which had become the top power plant of the turbo era, the Lotus-Senna combination could achieve no more than two wins. They were, in fact, the last this once all-conquering team ever achieved.

Autocourse wondered how Senna would make out at McLaren:

"It will be fascinating to see how such a natural driver will react to the inevitable and public comparison with Alain Prost…"

F1 WORLD CHAMPIONSHIP STANDINGS 1987

Position	Driver	Points
1	Nelson Piquet	73
2	Nigel Mansell	61
3	Ayrton Senna	57
4	Alain Prost	46
5	Gerhard Berger	36
6	Stefan Johansson	30
7	Michele Alboreto	17
8	Thierry Boutsen	16
9	Teo Fabi	12
10	Eddie Cheever	8
11	Jonathan Palmer	7
12	Satoru Nakajima	7
13	Riccardo Patrese	6
14	Andrea de Cesaris	4
15	Philippe Streiff	4
16	Derek Warwick	3
17	Philippe Alliot	3
18	Martin Brundle	2
19	Rene Arnoux	1
20	Ivan Capelli	1
21	Roberto Moreno	1

Satoru Nakajima & Ayrton Senna, Grand Prix of Hungary, Hungaroring, 1987

MAGNETI
MARELLI
GOODYEAR
John Player
Special
OLYMPUS
CAMERAS
elf

Ayrton Senna, Grand Prix of San Marino, Imola, 1986

Ayrton Senna with Gerard Ducarouge, Lotus-Renault 97T, Grand Prix of Italy, Monza, 1985

L: Ayrton Senna pictured during the 1987 British Grand Prix at Silverstone circuit, 1987

R: View of technical staff and mechanics working on the Camel Team Lotus Honda Lotus 99T Honda RA166E 1.5 V6 t racing car of Ayrton Senna, British Grand Prix at Silverstone circuit, 1987

Ayrton Senna racing his Camel Team Lotus Honda Lotus 99T Honda RA166E 1.5 V6t to finish in 3rd place in the 1987 British Grand Prix at Silverstone Circuit, England

LOTUS
LOTUS
HONDA
LOTUS
DeLonghi
DeLonghi
elf

Senna with the second-place trophy, Grand Prix of Brazil 1986

Thousands of Brazilians turned out to see Senna in his home Grand Prix

TRIPLE CHAMPION

C6

In his three years with Lotus, Ayrton Senna proved himself a race winner. But to be a champion, a top driver needs a top car. Senna would get his chance to compete for the World Drivers' Championship when he moved to the iconic red and white livery of McLaren in 1988 – but his first years there saw McLaren's two drivers descend into civil war.

The new decade saw Senna enjoy a champagne shower on many occasions

In its review of the 1987 season, the F1 annual Autocourse wondered how Ayrton Senna would make out as a McLaren driver. "*It will,***" the publication reflected, "***be fascinating to see how such a natural driver will react to the inevitable and public comparison with Alain Prost...***"**

Autocourse was not alone. Even though many people regarded Ayrton as the fastest driver in F1 others reckoned he would find Alain Prost a difficult team mate. Keke Rosberg, who partnered the Frenchman at McLaren in 1986, thought Lotus team principal Peter Warr had done Senna a big favour by persuading him to stay for another year in 1987, *"because the myth surrounding Ayrton would totally vanish next to Alain."*

Another of Prost's former team mates, John Watson, warned Senna that McLaren was also known as *"Team Prost."* According to his biographer, Christopher Hilton, *"Senna replied that he intended to beat Prost physically and mentally and at the first opportunity."* He was as good as his word. It was Prost not Senna who quit the team at the end of the following season amid one of the most bitter rivalries F1 had ever seen.

With a set of new F1 regulations due to take effect in 1989 the explosive turbo era was drawing to a close. Normally-aspirated 3.5-litre engines would replace the 1.5-litre turbos but cars with either type of engine were eligible in 1988. However, in an attempt to level the playing field, boost pressure and fuel capacity for the turbos would be drastically reduced.

During 1987 McLaren worked hard to convince Honda it was the right team to use its engines. Senna had formed a close association with Honda's management during his time at Lotus and, following the announcement at Monaco that he would be moving to McLaren for 1988, Senna joined Prost and Ron Dennis in a trip to Tokyo. The result was that the Japanese company agreed to transfer its supply of engines from Williams to McLaren. This was despite the departure to Ferrari of John Barnard, who designed McLaren's championship-winning TAG turbo cars.

But the timing of the decision meant that the 1988 car, the MP4/4, designed by a project group led by Steve Nicholls was a bit of a rush job. It was also a masterpiece of packaging, thanks partly to the smaller coolers and fuel tank now required. Motor Sport's Dennis Jenkinson noted approvingly: *"It was 'a designer's dream' for there was no need to make compromises to use anything from the 1987 cars. Everything could be designed from scratch and the whole car could be envisaged as a complete and integrated package."*

When the car ran in the last day of pre-season testing at Imola it was quickly apparent to the team that McLaren had created something special. *"I can't believe this car,"* Prost told team co-ordinator Jo Ramirez. *"It's absolutely fabulous."* Ron Dennis took Senna to one side and asked him to avoid showing the car's true potential to the other teams present. *"We'd just produced probably the best ever F1 grand prix car,"* Ramirez reflected.

It would become obvious soon enough that none of the competition was at the same level. McLaren would dominate the season to an extent not seen in F1, winning 15 out of the year's 16 races. Yet if it hadn't been for the intense competition that was to develop between Prost and Senna, 1988 would have been something of an anti-climax. As Jenkinson put it: *"McLaren is well aware that it is not really beating anyone of significance."*

In the end Senna would win eight races to Prost's seven. He would also set no fewer than 13 pole position times to Prost's two and, but for a regulation that allowed drivers to count only their best 11 points scores, the destination of the world championship would have been settled well before the end of the season.

Many years later Steve Nicholls reflected on his view of Senna's driving and what he put into it. *"There was a higher level of intensity with him,"* Nicholls said. *"All this stuff about the physical ability to drive the car, the intelligence and the feedback – on top of it all there's what I call the willingness factor. are you willing to go out there and let it all hang out? He had a little bit of an edge in that respect."*

Senna started the year at his home grand prix as he intended to go on, with pole position. But his gear lever stuck in first during the warm up lap so he switched to the spare car and started from the pit lane. But as he had done this after the green flag had been shown he had broken the rules and was subsequently black-flagged and disqualified. It was hardly a great start in front of his family, friends and legions of supporters.

He made amends at Imola with pole and a win ahead of Prost and a lap ahead of the third placed Lotus 100T of Piquet. According to Jenkinson, Senna took an *"unassailable lead before they reached the first corner."* His speed on the opening lap was *"breath-taking."* But at Monaco a *"minute error of judgement"* was enough to put him out of the race. Starting from another pole – an incredible second and a half better than Prost – the Brazilian jumped into the lead. He held it comfortably until the 67th of 78 laps. With Prost some way behind, Senna ignored Dennis' radioed entreaties to slow down. Going through Portier, his right front nose fin struck the apex, sending the car into the outside Armco wall and bending back the left front wheel and suspension.

It was, team co-ordinator Jo Ramirez thought, *"Ayrton Senna's biggest career mistake."* He got out of his car and strode back to his Monaco flat where for hours he refused to answer the phone. Eventually, Ramirez managed to speak to him. *"I must be the biggest idiot in the world,"* Senna sobbed down the line.

He was second to Prost in Mexico but returned to his winning ways with back-to-back victories in Canada and at Detroit, where Senna was, said Jenkinson, overcoming his dislike of long-haul air travel, *"perfection."* But in his home grand prix Prost was able to turn the ables on his team-mate. At Paul Ricard the French driver found the ideal set-up for his car and set a qualifying time that even Senna couldn't reach. He even matched the Brazilian in his incisive ability to pass slower cars as he lapped them to regain a lead lost to Senna.

At a very wet Silverstone, Ferrari monopolised the front row of the grid for once but in the race Senna asserted his wet-weather superiority with a dominant victory. Prost withdrew after 25 laps, saying conditions were so bad the race shouldn't have been started.

Senna won the next three races, in Germany (also wet), Hungary and Belgium, from pole with Prost following him home. But this pattern was about to be disrupted. From yet another pole Senna sprinted into the lead at Monza. The two McLarens then ran each other unexpectedly hard and, when Prost retired with engine trouble on lap 31, Senna was warned to ease off. Two laps from the end, with the Ferraris of Berger and Alboreto closing fast, he had barely enough fuel to finish the race. In his desire to stay ahead, Senna collided with a slower competitor he was trying to lap.

Senna was later criticised for not waiting until he'd negotiated the chicane to attempt a passing manoeuvre. Ramirez thought his impatience had lost the team its chance of a perfect score. Dennis lost a wager with F1 impresario Bernard Ecclestone who bet McLaren couldn't pull it off.

Even though Prost had already virtually conceded the title to his team mate, what might have been a turning point in the season came in the races on the Iberian Peninsula. At Estoril for the Portuguese Grand Prix, Prost seemed more confident, possibly because of a new chassis, but he started from pole and won. Senna, troubled by high fuel consumption, languished back in sixth. The early laps, though, saw a fierce duel between the two McLaren drivers. At one point, Prost forced Senna to put two wheels on the kerb. Senna retaliated by lunging at Prost, squeezing him so close to the pit wall that another team manager had to pull back his pit board to avoid striking Prost's helmet.

"The whole grand prix fraternity could hardly believe what they'd just seen," Jo Ramirez wrote later. In the team's motor home after the race quietly Prost told Senna that if he wanted the world championship that badly he could have it. Prost won again in Spain and although Senna gained his 11th pole position of the

Ayrton Senna in his McLaren-Honda MP4/4, Grand Prix of Hungary, Hungaroring, 1988

season, he could finish no higher than fourth, again troubled by high fuel consumption readings. Yet, going into the penultimate race, the Brazilian was effectively just five points behind the French driver – thanks to the scoring rules – and he could still settle matters in Japan.

Senna was back on form during qualifying but stalled his engine at the start. As the rest of the field surged around him he managed to get going thanks to the grid being on a slight slope. Prost was well away but after a blistering opening lap Senna had overtaken five cars and was up to eighth place. With 27 laps gone he was right on Prost's tail and when the Frenchman missed a gear he was through. By now, the drizzle which had started more than ten laps earlier, was making the track surface perilously slick. The gap between the two McLarens fluctuated but Prost seemed to have settled for second. At the finish he was over 13 sec behind.

After that the season-ending Australian grand prix seemed something of an anti- climax as Prost, determined to prevail in the final race of the turbo era, won comfortably from the new world champion. In truth, it had not been an easy race for either McLaren driver as both suffered gear selection problems. In addition, Prost's car was damaged when he ran over debris dropped by another car. Compensating for the altered handling meant higher tyre wear for the rest of the race.

Writing in Motor Sport after the Japanese Grand Prix, David Tremayne observed that, compared with Prost, Senna still had some things to learn. But, he added, "*as far as the title is concerned, the hungrier man won.*" But the seeds of disharmony between the two drivers had already been sown.....

Never mind the change to 3.5-Litre normally aspirated engines, put to one side the introduction of Honda's RA109E V10 engine in the back of the Neil Oatley-designed MP4/5 that enabled the Woking team to dominate another season, the main talking point of 1989 was the bust-up between the two McLaren drivers at Imola.

During the turbo era Senna had developed a distinctive driving technique for keeping the turbocharger spooled up while going through a corner. It was thought that the change to normally-aspirated engines would deprive him of this advantage but as events were to show, his car control and commitment more than compensated for it.

Yet, although McLaren was again comfortably victorious in the constructors' championship, it was not quite as dominant as in 1988. Senna took six wins to Prost's four but it was Prost who took the title, having scored points in 13 races. He was second six times. Senna, on the other hand, failed to score points on eight occasions and that included one when he was disqualified.

Although Senna and McLaren scored their first win of the year at San Marino this success was overshadowed by the row that broke out after the race. It transpired that Prost had agreed to Senna's suggestion that, from the start whoever was in front going into the Tosa corner would not be challenged until after the corner. Senna was first into Tosa at the start but the race was red flagged shortly afterwards when Gerhard Berger's Ferrari crashed and burst into flames.

At the re-start, Prost made the better get-away and, assuming that Senna would keep to their agreement, placed himself on the normal racing line for Tosa. But Senna passed him almost before he had started to brake for the corner. Prost was furious. After finishing behind the Brazilian, he stormed off without a word to anyone. Later, he told the journal L'Equipe that he'd felt betrayed and that Senna was not an honourable man.

This added further to the poisonous atmosphere

developing within the team and a week later Dennis summoned both drivers to a test session at the Pembrey circuit in South Wales where he read them the riot act. Under pressure, Senna apologised even though he maintained he'd done nothing wrong. From then on the two hardly spoke to one another and conversed mainly through their engineers.

Steve Nicholls recalled: "*Senna and Prost would debrief together but they didn't talk. Prost would ask his engineer a question – he wouldn't ask Senna. His engineer would ask me, I'd ask Senna, he'd tell me, I'd tell Prost's engineer and he'd tell Prost. But it worked and it was no problem. They had ultimate respect for each other. Senna would say to me: 'we don't have to worry about anyone else, just Alain.'*"

The struggle between the two driver continued unabated on track. Senna was victorious in Monaco and Mexico, while Prost won at Phoenix, Paul Ricard and Silverstone. Senna again failed to score points in his home race following a collision with Berger which sent him into the pits for a new nose. He suffered mechanical ills in the USA, France, Britain and Italy but won in the wet in Canada, Germany and Belgium and led McLaren one-twos at San Marino, Monaco, Hockenheim and Spa.

Yet by the time the teams reached Portugal, Senna was lagging 20 points behind his team mate in the championship table. Estoril was to do him no favours. Ferrari-mounted Nigel Mansell was black-flagged for reversing in the pit lane. Later he claimed that he hadn't seen the flag but when he attempted to pass Senna for the lead the two cars collided. It wasn't clear why Senna hadn't been warned that Mansell had been disqualified and that he could have let the Englishman pass.

As a result, Senna needed a win in Spain to keep his championship hopes alive. He duly delivered but it was all to no avail. Tensions were therefore running high when the McLaren team arrived at Suzuka for the Japanese Grand Prix, the penultimate race of the season. Senna started from pole but Prost had the better of the early laps and built a lead over the Brazilian. The gap varied but the duel had become an absorbing one by lap 47 – of 53 – by which time Senna was right behind his rival. Almost inevitably, the two cars collided when Senna tried to pass his rival at the chicane.

Prost vacated his car immediately but Senna gestured to the marshals to restart him down the escape road. He re-joined the circuit, pitted for a new nose cone and in the remaining few laps passed Alessandro Nannini who had taken the lead. Senna was disqualified for re-starting with outside assistance. This placed his team in the embarrassing position of protesting the disqualification of one of its runners following an incident which left the other as world champion.

Both drivers maintained they were in the right. In a press statement, Senna insisted: "*That was the only place where I could overtake. And somebody who should not have been there just closed the door and that was that.*" Jean-Marie Balestre, the self-important president of the FIA, motor sport's governing body, publicly blamed Senna for the accident. To McLaren team co-ordinator Jo Ramirez it was obvious that Prost had "*closed the door*" on his rival.

After the race Prost offered Senna his hand but the Brazilian declined to take it, saying he never wanted to see the Frenchman again. Ramirez wrote later that the incident "*completely finished*" any likelihood of personal relations between the two drivers being restored. There followed "*weeks of appeals, threats, counter-threats and press conferences.*" On top of the exclusion, Senna was fined $100,000 and given a six-month suspended

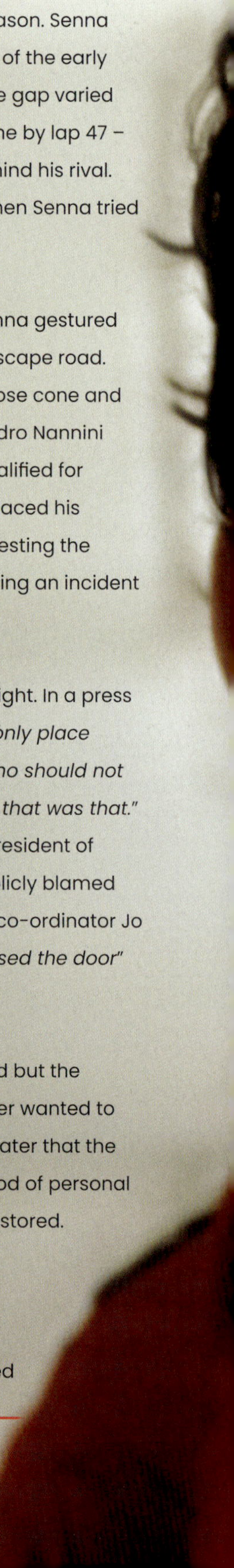

Ayrton Senna in a pensive moment in the pits before the Formula One United States Grand Prix March 1989

ban after accusing Balestre of manipulating the championship in Prost's favour.

The year's final race, the Australian Grand Prix, was run in torrential rain. Prost declined to start but Senna led the first 13 laps from pole position until he collided with another car in the atrocious conditions.

Going into the 1990 season there were doubts that Senna would be taking part but McLaren paid his fine and Senna agreed to apologise for his remarks. Meanwhile, Prost had left to join Ferrari and his place in the team had been taken by the affable Austrian Gerhard Berger. The Neil Oatley-designed MP4/5 was improved, as was its Honda V10 engine.

Senna's season started uncharacteristically with a fifth place on the grid for the US Grand Prix at Phoenix. A misfiring engine meant it was the first time since he had been off the front row of the grid since the 1988 British Grand Prix. Berger was on pole for his first race with the team but had to give way to his team mate who won after a tussle with Jean Alesi's nimble Tyrrell.

Senna was back on pole for his home race yet he was again denied his first Brazilian Grand Prix victory. "*Once again,*" observed Jo Ramirez, "*he was the victim of his own impatience.*" Leading Prost's Ferrari by 13 sec, he collided with the car he was lapping. A pit stop for a new nose meant a charge back through the field to third but it was Prost who took the win.

A damaged wheel rim put Senna out of the San Marino race but he was in a class of his own at Monte Carlo setting pole position and taking fastest lap as well as victory in a race which had to be started twice.

Ayrton Senna & Alain Prost in their McLaren-Honda MP4/5s, Grand Prix of Monaco, 1990

He also won the Canadian Grand Prix but then came a sequence of Prost victories, in Mexico, France and Britain.

Mexico was Senna's 100th grand prix but the celebratory cake presented by his team was his only reward. He failed to win pole position – taken by Berger – and then he suffered a late race puncture which put him out of contention. So by the time the team arrived at Hockenheim for the German Grand Prix Prost was leading the championship by two points. Senna won from pole but was made to work hard for it by Nannini who had made his Benetton's tyres last and thereby avoid a pit stop.

In Hungary Senna was forced to spend his whole race staring at the gearbox of Boutsen's Williams-Renault on this twisty circuit which didn't encourage overtaking. But McLaren was buoyed up by the ten point championship lead Senna was able to take to Spa for the Belgian Grand Prix. Opening lap accidents meant that the race had to be started three times, but Senna was again supreme to the great satisfaction of Dennis Jenkinson. *"....the fact that there are few drivers who can challenge Ayrton Senna and few cars that can match the McLaren-Honda V10 is unfortunate from the racing point of view but does not detract from the joy of watching a master driver in action,"* he wrote in his Motor Sport report of the race.

The bearded scribe had plenty to cheer about at Monza, too. Indeed, such was Senna's eleventh-hour pole-setting lap following an engine change that Jenkinson said he could have packed up and gone home *"because anything else was going to be an anti-climax."* In his Autocourse report, Alan Henry observed

Shell
BOSS

that Senna's win over Prost meant he was going to need *"a great deal of bad luck if he was not to take the second world championship of his career."*

At the post-race press conference an Italian journalist persuaded the two drivers to bury the hatchet. After what Jo Ramirez described as *"a very tense moment,"* they shook hands and slapped each other on the back." As a rapprochement, though, it was to be a short-lived one.

Senna came away from the Portuguese and Spanish grands prix with one second place and a retirement. More to the point, the gap to Prost in the world championship had shrunk to just nine points. So it was that the scene shifted back to Suzuka where the previous year the title chase had been ended by a collision and followed by months of acrimony. It couldn't happen again, could it?

Although the circuit suited Prost's Ferrari, Senna secured pole position. But this didn't please him as he considered it would put him not on the racing line but on the inside of the track where the surface offered less grip. The race officials declined to change the grid.

Senna, already tense, walked out of the drivers' pre-race briefing when officials seemed unclear about what would happen to drivers unable to negotiate the chicane where he and Prost had collided the year before. *"It was then I realised that he was capable of doing whatever was necessary to secure the title,"* Jo Ramirez recalled. *"Two hours later the championship was decided in 400m and just a few seconds."*

As expected, Prost made a better start from the outside of the front row and was first to the next corner. But Senna, on the inside, refused to lift and with almost two wheels on the grass the nose of the McLaren hit the gearbox of the Ferrari. Both cars ended in the gravel trap. *"I couldn't believe my eyes,"* Ramirez wrote, *"what a terrible way to finish the championship!"*

The result, according to Maurice Hamilton's Autocourse report, was that Senna had become champion *"by the simple expedient of having assisted the immediate departure of his rival."* Prost launched a withering attack on his rival's ethics, claiming he'd been pushed off the track. *"Senna would have none of it,"* Hamilton reported, *"and the day degenerated into a morass of bitterness and self-righteous indignation."*

"Anybody can make a mistake," observed Alan Henry," *but the manner in which Ayrton denied any responsibility for the incident was seen as quite extraordinary by many dispassionate observers."*

Once again, with the championship decided, the season finale in Australia was robbed of much of its significance. Senna started from pole position but although he led much of the race he was forced to retire when, with less than 20 laps to run, gear selection problems caused him to slide off into a barrier.

The 1991 season was, by Senna's standards, relatively calm. He secured his third world championship with seven wins and eight poles compared with the five wins and two poles of runner-up Nigel Mansell. But it was becoming clear to Senna that the Williams with its Renault V10 engine was becoming the combination to beat. Even the new McLaren MP4/6 chassis with V12 Honda engine and a string of early victories couldn't hide the writing that he saw was all-too clearly on the wall.

While Senna seemed to have matured as a driver

Ayrton Senna, Grand Prix of Japan, Suzuka, 1990

and to have lost some of the impulsiveness that had characterised his earlier years, his contest with Mansell seemed no less intense than those with Prost. Some of the images from the season captured some of the excitement. In one, the two men are side-by-side at 200 mph in the Spanish Grand Prix, their cars throwing up showers of sparks; another, showing the victorious Mansell giving the stranded Senna a lift on the sidepod of his Williams at the British Grand Prix received wide exposure.

As it happened, though, the Silverstone incident hinted at the serious fuel consumption problem which McLaren and Honda were having to grapple with. The same problem put Senna out of the German Grand Prix run on championship decider but not in the way it had been in 1989 and 1990, although Senna's clear-cut and cleanly-won title were undermined by his post-race outburst against the FIA and its president. During the race Mansell spun out to destroy his hopes of winning the title which Senna clinched by finishing second to his team-mate Berger.

Any hopes that, for the first time in three years, the Japanese race could be conducted in an atmosphere free of rancour were dashed by Senna's utterances at the post-race press conference when he unleashed a venomous attack on Jean-Marie Balestre. "*As his pent-up emotions spilled over, Senna boldly admitted that he had deliberately pushed Alain Prost off the*

F1 WORLD CHAMPIONSHIP STANDINGS 1988

Position	Driver	Points
1	**Ayrton Senna**	**90**
2	Alain Prost	87
3	Gerhard Berger	41
4	Thierry Boutsen	27
5	Michele Alboreto	24
6	Nelson Piquet	22
7	Ivan Capelli	17
8	Derek Warwick	17
9	Nigel Mansell	12
10	Alessandro Nannini	12
11	Riccardo Patrese	8
12	Eddie Cheever	6
13	Mauricio Gugelmin	5
14	Jonathan Palmer	5
15	Andrea de Cesaris	3
16	Pierluigi Martini	1
17	Satoru Nakajima	1

F1 WORLD CHAMPIONSHIP STANDINGS 1989

Position	Driver	Points
1	Alain Prost	76
2	**Ayrton Senna**	**60**
3	Riccardo Patrese	40
4	Nigel Mansell	38
5	Thierry Boutsen	37
6	Alessandro Nannini	32
7	Gerhard Berger	21
8	Nelson Piquet	12
9	Jean Alesi	8
10	Derek Warwick	7
11	Eddie Cheever	6
12	Stefan Johansson	6
13	Michele Alboreto	6
14	Johnny Herbert	5
15	Pierluigi Martini	5
16	Mauricio Gugelmin	4
17	Andrea de Cesaris	4
18	Stefano Modena	4
19	Alex Caffi	4
20	Martin Brundle	4
21	Satorou Nakajima	3
22	Christian Danner	3
23	Emanuele Pirro	2
24	Rene Arnoux	2
25	Jonathan Palmer	2
26	Olivier Grouillard	1
27	Gabriele Tarquini	1
28	Luiz Perez-Sala	1
29	Philippe Alliot	1

Ayrton Senna in his McLaren-Honda MP4/6, Grand Prix of Portugal, Autodromo do Estoril, 1991

F1 WORLD CHAMPIONSHIP STANDINGS 1990

Position	Driver	Points
1	**Ayrton Senna**	**78**
2	Alain Prost	71
3	Nelson Piquet	43
4	Gerhard Berger	43
5	Nigel Mansell	37
6	Thierry Boutsen	34
7	Riccardo Patrese	23
8	Alessandro Nannini	21
9	Jean Alesi	13
10	Ivan Capelli	6
11	Roberto Moreno	6
12	Aguri Suzuki	6
13	Eric Bernard	5
14	Satoru Nakajima	3
15	Derek Warwick	3
16	Alex Caffi	2
17	Stefano Moreno	2
18	Mauricio Gugelmin	1

F1 WORLD CHAMPIONSHIP STANDINGS 1991

Position	Driver	Points
1	**Ayrton Senna**	**96**
2	Nigel Mansell	72
3	Riccardo Patrese	53
4	Gerhard Berger	43
5	Alain Prost	34
6	Nelson Piquet	26.5
7	Jean Alesi	21
8	Stefano Modena	10
9	Andrea de Cesaris	9
10	Roberto Moreno	8
11	Pierluigi Martini	6
12	J J Lehto	4
13	Bertrand Gachot	4
14	Michael Schumacher	4
15	Satoru Nakajima	2
16	Mika Hakkinen	2
17	Martin Brundle	2
18	Emanuele Pirro	1
19	Mark Blundell	1
20	Ivan Capelli	1
21	Eric Bernard	1
22	Aguri Suzuki	1
23	Julian Bailey	1
24	Gianni Morbidelli	0.5

Shell
BOSS

Ayrton Senna prepares to get in his Formula One Car at the 1990 San Marino Grand Prix, Imola, Italy

Ayrton Senna and Alain Prost confer with team principal Ron Dennis during their second qualifying practice, Grand Prix of Japan 1988

Ayrton Senna driving for the McLaren-Ford team during the Italian Grand Prix, 1991

Ayrton Senna driving a Honda Marlboro McLaren McLaren MP4/6 Honda RA121E 3.5 V12, is surrounded by his pit crew during testing in Jerez, Spain, 1991

Marlboro
POWERED by HONDA
Marlboro
Shell
Marlboro
Shell
COURTAULDS
Marlboro
Marlboro
Marlboro
Marlboro

Senna shares a joke with new teammate Gerhard Berger, 1990 pre-season testing

Not for the first time, Senna was a master of the wet in Britain in 1988

FOSTER'S
FOSTER'S
CAMPAR

RACING INTO HISTORY

C7

Senna kisses the kerb, Grand Prix of Monaco 1992

It's tough to get to the top. It's even tougher to stay there. After a golden period under Alain Prost and Ayrton Senna, McLaren no longer boasted the fastest cars on the grid. Instead, they belonged to the Williams team driven by Nigel Mansell and Ricardo Patrese – and a year later, Senna's old rival, Prost. Eventually, Senna would switch to Williams too, but his attempts to remain competitive had a tragic end.

Going into the 1992 F1 season it was obvious that the dominant team would be Williams-Renault and not McLaren-Honda which had been top dog for the previous four seasons.

Not that Ayrton Senna ever stopped trying. But it was not until the season was almost one-third run that he was able to mount the top step of the podium. And although he repeated this feat twice more he had to be content with fourth place in the world championship.

Senna and Berger had to wait until the Brazilian Grand Prix for the new MP4/7A with its Honda RA122E V12 engine. For the first two races of the year they'd had to rely on the previous year's MP4/6B. Speaking to the press before his home race, Senna revealed that the new car had been delayed by the effort required to catch and beat Williams-Renault at the end of 1991. "*We are now in a very difficult position,*" he admitted.

So far in 1992 he had scored one hard-fought third place, in South Africa. But retirement in Mexico (on lap 9 due to transmissions problems) was followed by a DNF in Brazil with the new car. This time he lasted 16 laps before electrical trouble intervened. He had been battling with rising German star Michael Schumacher for third place.

An improved MP4/7A with revised engine electronics and computer mapping appeared in Spain, but Senna still found himself out-qualified by Schumacher in the V8 Ford-powered Benetton. In the race he made a good start but was passed by Schumacher and pressed by Berger. "*If ever a driver has suffered an unexpected reversal of fortune of late,*" remarked Motor Sport, "*it is the world champion.*" Towards the end of the race it started to rain and, as the conditions worsened, Senna spun off into retirement. "*The conditions were very difficult, especially during the last 10 or 15 laps,*" he said later.

At San Marino Senna finished third but he had to work so hard for it that, by the end of the race, according to Motor Sport, he was close to physical collapse. By the time the teams arrived at Monte Carlo in May Nigel Mansell had posted five wins – a perfect score – in the actively-suspended Williams-Renault.

Senna qualified third behind the two Williams-Renaults and at the start was able to catapult his MP4/7A into second place ahead of Riccardo Patrese. For 71 laps Senna sat behind Mansell but when the Englishman dived into his pit to fix what turned out to be a loose wheel nut, Senna inherited a lead he was determined to keep no matter what Mansell did. By the finish he was just 0.2 sec to the good to score a victory against the odds that had required luck and good judgement.

"*For the last five or six laps,*" Senna said later, "*I had nothing left to give. My tyres were finished and I knew Nigel would catch me on fresh tyres so I gave it everything. All I could do was try and stay on the road and in the right place.*"

In Canada Senna jumped into an early lead from pole position with Mansell right behind him and, again, trying everything he knew to get past. In his Motor Sport report, David Tremayne wrote that in the early laps "*Senna was driving one of his supremely confident tactically defensive races.*" It was, Tremayne added: "*Gripping stuff because you never knew who or what was going to crack first.....*"

It turned out to be Mansell. A desperate lunge down the inside of Senna going in to the final chicane put the Williams-Renault off the circuit and out of the race. Senna maintained his lead until lap 36 (of 69) when his engine simply cut out.

There were two further retirements, in France and Britain, before things started to look up for Senna. At Silverstone he had scrapped with his old F3 sparring partner Martin

Brundle before his transmission failed, but at Magny-Cours Senna and Schumacher collided at the start. At Hockenheim Senna realised that his best chance of success lay in looking after his tyres and avoiding a stop for new rubber. The ploy worked despite pressure from Patrese. "*The last ten laps were very worrying because I had bad vibrations from my tyres,*" Senna said later.

Thanks to a good start, luck and canny judgement, the Brazilian scored his second victory of the season on the tight and twisty Hungaroring. It was, said Motor Sport's Tremayne "*an excellent 35th victory.*" From third place on the grid Senna jumped ahead of Mansell and then took the lead shortly afterwards. He had to resist fierce pressure for the rest of the race. "*I think I'm driving as well as ever in my career,*" Senna said afterwards. "*The sort of performance today is the product of experience. I did not expect to win.*"

His last victory of the year came at Monza. It followed a gamble over tyres in wet conditions at Spa that didn't come off. The Italian victory was a fortuitous one made possible by the failure of the Williams-Renaults but the Brazilian made his own luck by continuing to run as hard as he could and exploiting the McLaren's reliability.

Luck also played a part in Senna's third place in Portugal when he had to make three tyre stops. "*The car went completely mad over the last few laps,*" he reported later. "*At the finish I had a deflated tyre.*" In Japan, the MP4/7 was out after two laps with engine problems, while his Australian Grand Prix was cut short by a collision with Mansell after an intense scrap for the lead. The season therefore ended with Senna fourth in the world championship with less than half Mansell's points tally. In fact, he finished three points behind Schumacher.

If 1992 was a difficult year for McLaren, 1993 should have been even more so. At the Italian Grand Prix Honda had announced its withdrawal from F1, obliging McLaren to use the Cosworth HB V8 engine. But it was a customer unit because Benetton, as the Ford works team, took priority. According to McLaren team co-ordinator Jo Ramirez, "*Through the whole season there was a political struggle to get the same engines as Benetton, even though we were winning more often than they were.*"

Senna, meanwhile, was keen on a move to Williams-Renault with which, he believed, he could win a fourth title. When the seat went to Prost, who had taken a sabbatical during 1992, it seemed possible that Brazilian would quit McLaren, forcing the team had to nominate another driver in his place. For a while, indeed, Senna even talked about leaving F1 to race in the USA. He was, however, persuaded to try the new MP4/8 and was impressed by it. "*I knew it had tremendous potential,*" he said. But he still wouldn't commit to driving for the team for the whole season and didn't do so until it was nearly half over. Initially, he and Ron Dennis had agreed a race-by-race deal but Senna's demands, Ramirez recalled, "*were far higher than McLaren could meet.*" The result was that the team's commercial director, Ekrem Sami, was "*in overdrive*" negotiating additional sponsorship deals.

Was it worth it? Senna's performances in a car significantly inferior to the Williams-Renault probably did more than any others to cement his reputation as one of F1 greatest-ever drivers. The new season started well enough with a worthy second place in South Africa behind Prost's Williams-Renault but he was able to snatch victory in Brazil. Rain altered the whole complexion of a race that had been dominated initially by the two Williams. But Senna's wet weather ability enabled him to score what Motor Sport called "*another brilliant win made all the sweeter by virtue of being on his home ground.*"

Then came what many observers feel is still Senna's greatest-ever win. A poll of Autosport readers conducted in 2017 revealed that his victory in the European Grand Prix at Donnington Park represented the greatest wet weather drive ever. The magazine itself commented: *"There is no doubting Donnington was one of the great F1 drives of all time and is one of the most well-known wins in the wet."*

What particularly caught spectators' imagination was Senna's opening lap, which is considered one of the greatest ever seen in F1. At the start, Prost and Hill got away well in their Williams-Renaults. Senna was crowded out and dropped to fifth behind a fast-starting Karl Wendlinger (up to third) and Schumacher. But he quickly disposed of Schumacher and went round the outside of Wendlinger through the Craner Curves. Two corners later he was past Hill for second before taking the lead from Prost at the hairpin.

In his Motor Sport report David Tremayne called it *"annihilation." "Frankly,"* he wrote, *"it made the rest of them look as if they were still on their warm-up lap."* Thereafter, changeable conditions played to Senna's strengths and by the end he'd lapped everybody except the second-placed Hill. *"If I don't race again I feel comfortable with this,"* was Senna's post-race verdict on his performance. Jo Ramirez thought his opening laps *"were the best in modern F1 history."* He added: *"With weather conditions changing all the time it was an inspired drive by Ayrton which I'll never forget."*

Even though Prost won the next race in Imola, from which Senna retired due to hydraulic system failure, the Frenchman was still lagging behind the Brazilian in the championship table. But the positions were reversed in Spain following another Prost victory. Senna was second after a race of attrition and difficulty lapping slower runners. *"The back-markers were really terrible,"* he grumbled later.

Prost was judged to have jumped the start at Monte Carlo

Ayrton Senna in his McLaren-Honda MP4/7A, Grand Prix of Monaco, 1992

for which he was required to serve a stop-go penalty and this helped Senna to win his fifth consecutive Monaco despite a practice accident which could have been more serious than it was. "*After my accident,*" he said later, "*I knew I had lost my edge because the difference going flat out here and going 99 per cent is big. And in that shunt I lost the 100 per cent possibility. I was thinking hard before going to bed on Saturday and when I got up on race morning I was thinking positively. Prost jumped the start, perhaps in desperation to get to the first corner, a result of the pressure I exerted even though I was behind him.*"

As it happened, it was Schumacher, second on the grid, who took an early lead which he lost due to hydraulic problems on lap 33 out of 78. Senna assumed the lead and commanded the race to the end despite a stop for tyres. "*All I thought about,*" he said after the race, "*was keeping my concentration. I know how you can lose it here.*"

The next eight races yielded little for Senna beyond three fourth places and a fifth as the William-Renault drivers scored seven wins between them. But the rest of the season belonged to the Brazilian as he achieved what would be his final grand prix victories. In Japan he put in another "*mesmerising drive,*" according to Jo Ramirez, to win his fourth grand prix of the year, while in Australia he won on his final outing for McLaren.

Changeable weather at Suzuka played into his hands and he won the Japanese Grand Prix by over 40 sec from Prost despite three stops for tyre changes. He led from his front row grid position but had to pit for a new set of slicks on the 13th lap. Seven laps later the rain started and, after a flurry of changes to wets, Senna emerged in the lead looking very comfortable in the dire conditions. A return to drier conditions meant a further tyre change but Senna was able to keep his lead.

But it seemed that he couldn't leave Suzuka without being involved in controversy. This time the target of Senna's anger was Eddie Irvine who was having his first F1 drive with the Jordan team. Senna was still on wets by lap 34 (of 53). By that time the rain had eased and a dry line was emerging as Senna came up to lap a gaggle of cars led by Irvine. Senna passed but Irvine re-passed and continued to try and stay ahead of the Brazilian who couldn't make his move stick until lap 37. By that time his lead over Prost had been halved.

When Senna sought out Irvine after the race the cocky Ulsterman was unrepentant and unmoved by the tirade that burst over him. Clearly irritated by his insouciance, Senna punched him. "*Irvine drove like a great idiot today,*" Senna fumed. "*He was quick, sure, but this is F1 not go-karts.*" Irvine said: "*I was just going as quickly as I could in the conditions.*" Motor Sport's David Tremayne wasn't impressed. He saw the Brazilian's assault on Irvine as a "*fall from grace*" for Senna, who had always enjoyed great popularity in Japan. In Australia, Tremayne reported, Senna found a pair of boxing gloves in his MP4/8's cockpit.

Emotions were running high at Adelaide, for the Australian Grand Prix was Prost's F1 swansong as well as Senna's final race in a McLaren. On the grid – he was in pole position – he told Jo Ramirez: "*It's a very strange feeling for me to do this for the last time in a McLaren.*" The Mexican replied: "*If you win this one for us I'll love you forever.*" He recalled later: "*Ayrton grabbed my arm very hard and I saw tears in his eyes.*"

Senna led from the start and began pulling away from Prost so that by lap 10 his lead was over 3 sec. Prost took over briefly when Senna stopped for tyres but by two-thirds distance the gap had gone out to nearly 30 sec. At the flag it was just over 9 sec. On the podium, Senna and Prost shook hands, something the Brazilian had pointedly declined to do in Japan. "*Ayrton was pleasant and warm,*" recalled Jo Ramirez, "*maybe because it was his idea or because Prost was no longer his worst 'enemy' on the track.*"

»

Ayrton Senna and Michael Schumacher are separated during a dispute at the French Grand Prix

Marlboro
Marlboro
Marlboro
BOSS
Shell
COURTAULDS

In its annual assessment of Senna, Autocourse thought he might claim to be the best driver of his era even though his *"level of achievement varied more dramatically in 1993 than ever before."* The publication noted: *"His wins at Interlagos, Donnington Park and Suzuka served to confirm his matchless genius in the wet and his victory at Adelaide was surely the most decisive success achieved by anybody all year."*

His confrontation with Eddie Irvine, however, combined with his attitude to the British media for what he saw as an over-critical attitude towards him as a result, *"provided yet another disturbing insight into Senna's extraordinarily intense egocentricity and uniquely flawed genius."*

For Senna and McLaren, 1993 marked the end of an era during which they had together scored three drivers' titles, 35 grand prix wins, 47 pole positions and 447 world championship points. Desperate to have the Renault power which had propelled Mansell and Prost to the last two world championships, Senna had signed to drive for Williams for 1994.

It was said that Prost had opted to retire rather than face being Senna's team-mate again. Whatever the truth of this, the two-year deal had been done on 14 September, two days after the Italian Grand Prix at Monza and many observers believed Senna was now on his way to a fourth world championship. When he visited the Williams factory at Didcot, chief designer Adrian Newey showed him round. He was impressed with Senna's *"interest in detail, his inquisitiveness and his obvious enthusiasm."* In the wind tunnel he was shown a model of his 1994 car and Newey noted the driver's keenness to understand the design and philosophy of the car. *"A desire to learn,"* Newey recalled, *"it was definitely one of the qualities that made him so great."* He added: *"The thought of working with him was tremendously exciting."*

Senna had his first taste of the car at an uncharacteristically chilly Estoril in January. The next day, looking unfamiliar in Rothmans blue in place of the familiar Marlboro red and white, Senna made a demonstration run watched by around 350 journalists and posed for photographers with his new team-mate, Damon Hill.

Yet those who'd seen the Williams-Renault-Senna combination as so strong that it would sweep the board were having second thoughts. Electronic driver aids like traction control and active suspension which had become such an integral part of the most successful were now banned and their removal initially brought some difficult and unpredictable handling.

Senna himself was becoming uneasy about the FW16 saying he didn't feel comfortable in it at Estoril despite changes to the position of the seat and steering wheel. *"Some of that is down to the lack of electronic change,"* he said. Team mate Hill shared his feelings. *"The car was not the beauty we wanted it to be and Ayrton was concerned that he couldn't push it as much as he needed to,"* he observed.

The season began in Brazil on 27 March. Senna set pole position and led Michael Schumacher's Benetton until they made their pit stops after which the positions were reversed. Then, while he was harrying the German driver, Senna spun out of the race, admitting it was his fault. He was again on pole for the Pacific Grand Prix at Aida, Japan on 17 April and again he failed to finish. This time he was nudged off the track minutes after the start. In both cases, the race was won by Schumacher.

Newey worked hard to revise the FW16 in time for the San Marino Grand Prix with aerodynamic and other changes designed to improve driver comfort. Whether or not it would be enough remained to be seen. Senna put the car on pole but the tone for the week-end was inadvertently set by his countryman, Rubens Barrichello. His Jordan

Senna during the 1993 Monaco Grand Prix

Rothmans
Rothmans
RACING

somersaulted after clipping the kerb at 140 mph entering the tricky Variante Bassa S-bend during Friday practice. Barrichello was lucky to escape with superficial injuries but during the following day's qualification the Austrian driver Roland Ratzenberger crashed fatally after the nose section of his car became detached and he lost control.

Senna was always upset by accidents involving fellow drivers but the was his first experience of a fatality. He was told of Ratzenberger's death by the eminent neurosurgeon and F1 doctor Professor Sid Watkins with whom he had formed a close friendship.. *"Ayrton broke down and cried on my shoulder,"* Watkins recalled. He felt Senna was so upset that he was in no condition to race. *"In fact,"* he asked his friend, *"why don't you give it up altogether? Give it up and let's go fishing."*

But Senna told him: *"Sid, there are certain things over which we have no control. I can't quit. I have to go on."* Watkins wrote later: *"Those were the last words he ever said to me."* But Watkins, like others at Imola that week-end, couldn't shake off a feeling of doom.

At the start of the race the next day a collision between two cars meant that the pace car had to be deployed. When it came in and the cars were released to resume racing Watkins, in the medical car following the tail of the field told his driver Mario Casoni: *"There's going to be a fucking awful accident any minute."*

In his autobiography Life at the Limit Watkins describes the sequence of events. *"The next moment the red flags were out again. Casoni took off and, as we approached Tamburello, somehow I knew it was Senna,"* he wrote. When the safety car came in, Senna timed his restart to perfection so that by the end of the sixth lap he was 0.6 sec ahead of Schumacher as he hurtled into Tamburello. Then, suddenly, the Williams twitched, lurched to the right and slammed into the concrete retaining wall.

Watkins found Senna slumped in his cockpit. *"His eyes were closed and he was deeply unconscious,"* Watkins recalled. *"He looked serene. I raised his eyelids and it was clear from his pupils that he had a massive brain injury. We lifted him from the cockpit and laid him on the ground. As we did he sighed and, though I am totally agnostic, I felt his soul departed at that moment."*

The race was red-flagged but re-started 37 minutes after the crash. It was not until 18:40 hr, more than two hours after the race had finished, that Senna was officially pronounced dead.

Although Michael Schumacher won the San Marino Grand Prix and went on to seal the 1994 world championship, he considered that, but for Ayrton Senna's fatal accident the Brazilian would almost certainly have wrapped up the title for himself and probably by the Italian Grand Prix.

The man the German driver beat to the title, by one point, was Senna's team mate Damon Hill. In a way, history repeated itself. In 1968, following the death of Jim Clark, Hill's father Graham had found himself leading a totally demoralised team. Now Damon found himself in a similar position. Just like his father had done he even scored a morale-boosting win in the Spanish Grand Prix.

Of course, no-one can say that Senna would have gone on to win the `95 title had he survived but it's known that

Grand Prix of Pacific, Okayama International Circuit, 1994

he harboured a desire to drive for Ferrari. Just four days before he died, he's reported to have had a two-hour telephone conversation with Ferrari president Luca di Montezemolo during which the Brazilian is believed to have discussed the possibility of joining the Italian team in 1996.

As it was, the drivers observed a minute's silence in honour of Senna and Ratzenberger at the start of the next race, the Monaco Grand Prix. For European F1 fans Senna's death was a body-blow but nothing compared to the sense of loss felt in his home country. His successes had given Brazilians a sense of dignity and recognition to the extent that he was lionised as a national hero.

On arrival at Sao Paulo his coffin was immediately taken to the state legislature building for a ceremonial lying in state. More than 250,000 people lined the route. Ayrton Senna was buried the next day amid scenes usually associated with heads of state.

Meanwhile, in accordance with Italian law, his FW16 was impounded by the authorities. The subsequent investigation focused on the car's steering column. It was broken and showed signs of having been cut and welded. This emerged as the key issue: had the breakage caused the crash or resulted from it?

For Adrian Newey there were other considerations. Although he didn't think the steering column was responsible for the accident, Newey felt that he'd *"screwed up the aerodynamics of the car."* In his autobiography, How to Build a Car, Newey wrote: *"I messed up the transition from active suspension back to passive and designed a car that was aerodynamically unstable, in which Ayrton attempted to do things the car was not capable of."* Newey was certain that by Imola he'd understood the problem and just needed time *"to give Ayrton a car that was worthy of him."* But, he added: *"Time denied us all that chance."*

Meanwhile, the threat of prosecution hung over Frank Williams, Patrick Head and Newey until it was eventually lifted in 2007. In 1997 the case against the defendants had been found not proven but three years later the matter

F1 WORLD CHAMPIONSHIP STANDINGS 1992

Position	Driver	Points
1	Nigel Mansell	108
2	Riccardo Patrese	56
3	Michael Schumacher	53
4	**Ayrton Senna**	**50**
5	Gerhard Berger	49
6	Martin Brundle	38
7	Jean Alesi	18
8	Mika Hakkinen	11
9	Andrea de Cesaris	8
10	Michele Alboreto	6
11	Erik Comas	4
12	Karl Wendlinger	3
13	Ivan Capelli	3
14	Thierry Boutsen	2
15	Johnny Herbert	2
16	Pierluigi Martini	2
17	Stefano Modena	1
18	Christian Fittipaldi	1
19	Bertrand Gachot	1

F1 WORLD CHAMPIONSHIP STANDINGS 1993

Grand Prix of South-Africa, Kyalami, 1992

Ayrton Senna's McLaren-Honda MP4/7A being worked on in the pits at the Grand Prix of Canada, Circuit Gilles Villeneuve, 1992

Marlboro
WORLD CHAMPIONSHIP TEAM
Marlboro
GOODYEAR
EAGLE

Rothmans
RENAULT
Segafredo
ZANETTI

Grand Prix of Pacific, TI Circuit, Aida, 1994

Ayrton Senna in action in his Williams Renault during the Formula One testing at the Estoril circuit in Portugal, 1994

Clouds over Senna at Silverstone, Grand Prix of Britain 1992

Old foe Alain Prost was on the podium when Senna recorded the final win of his career, Australian Grand Prix 1993

TERS
GOODYEAR
Marlboro
Marlboro
McLAREN INTERNATIONAL

A COMPLEX MAN

Senna didn't score a point for Williams but earned pole position in all three races for the team

Ayrton Senna's early death shook the world of motorsport. Two decades earlier, racing fatalities were common, but by the mid-1990s, Formula 1 had radically improved safety. Nobody expected the death of a driver – never mind two in the same weekend. Obituaries were hastily written. Senna's legacy was judged. Fans and pundits mourned the loss of a driver who had achieved so much – and perhaps would have done even more.

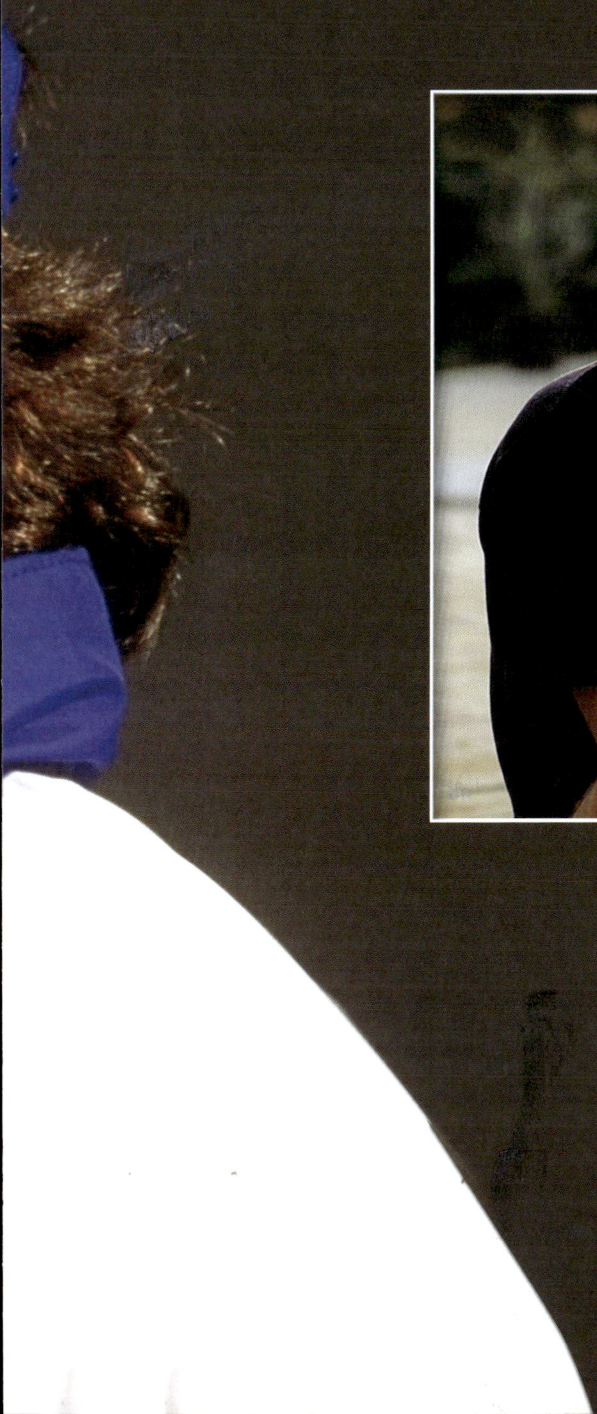

Senna at home in his native Brazil

C8

Some people thought him arrogant and aloof, while others saw him as a warm and friendly chap who enjoyed a laugh. Clearly, as befitted a man once described as the most complex character on the F1 grid, there were several Ayrton Sennas and, inevitably a mass of contradictions.

One who thought so was Martin Brundle. F1 competitor and 1983 F3 sparring partner, Brundle believed Senna's interest in safety was laced with a high degree of self-interest: "*There was always a great paradox with Ayrton.*" Brundle acknowledged that at the Imola medical centre following Rubens Barrichello's 1994 accident Senna had "*shown great compassion.*" But, Brundle pointed out, "*strangely, he would also be one of the first to have an accident with you or push you off the road.*"

Even the feud with Alain Prost which defined Senna's most successful years in F1 may not have been quite as it seemed. When Prost retired at the end of 1993 he stopped being a threat to Senna and his aspirations. Prost even believed Senna's motivation changed. At Imola in `94 Prost was commentating on the race for a French TV channel. Senna had arranged to send an on-air message to "*our dear friend, Alain*" during his warming up lap: "*We all miss you, Alain.*" Prost is convinced the message was sincere.

Of course, Senna's benchmark had also gone. One thing great F1 drivers have in common is the ability to be in the best car run by the best team and then mould that team around themselves. Fangio did it and so did Schumacher. Senna ended his first season with McLaren as world champion but was well aware that, but for a quirk in the points scoring system, he'd probably have ended up as runner-up to Prost. By the end of his second season he had transformed McLaren from Team Prost to Team Senna.

Whether he deliberately engineered it or not, the dispute which erupted between the two men at Imola in `89 and exploded later at Suzuka resulted in Prost feeling that after six years he was no longer comfortable at Woking. Although he left McLaren for Ferrari that didn't end the feud between them because Prost remained Senna's greatest rival.

The 1990 championship was again settled at Suzuka, this time in Senna's favour, but in a manner that horrified many F1 followers. His lack of remorse and subsequent utterances also outraged the governing body and its president, Jean-Marie Balestre, to such an extent that, for a while, the Brazilian's continued presence on the F1 stage was in doubt.

Lotus team principal Peter Warr thought it was Senna's innate honesty that got him into so much trouble and created misunderstandings. "*Throughout he was true to his principles,*" Warr believed. "*One of the first of those principles was honesty with himself and everybody else.*" Warr also thought Senna also had a strong sense of injustice which, away from F1, found expression in his determination to ease the plight of underprivileged children in Brazil.

There were certainly two sides to having a driver of Senna's calibre on your side as the teams he drove for quickly discovered. Warr felt that Senna's presence galvanised the team to put in the additional effort needed to achieve a target or gain an additional edge. Suppliers suddenly became eager to deliver on time and negotiations with sponsors were easier. "*Even the bank manager seems more approachable and amenable,*" Warr noted. "*Pride goes up by leaps and bounds and everything that seems difficult and tiresome about F1 somehow becomes easier to tolerate. Ayrton brought these special strengths in abundance and transformed the fortunes of Team Lotus.*"

Yet with Senna there was always the unspoken threat: give me a car I can win the world championship with or I'll walk.

Sir Stirling Moss counted himself an admirer. *"Many accepted the image of a man constantly at war with his rivals and preferred to choose more peaceful, more equable heroes,"* he observed. *"Ayrton could be difficult and he did occasionally do foolish things. But then men who care often do."* Moss added: *"He was totally loyal to his friends and his family. He was honest to an unusual degree. And he could be touchingly kind, particularly to the younger drivers."*

In 1990 Sir Jackie Stewart, who had spent much of his active career campaigning for greater F1 safety, conducted a TV interview with Senna in which he pointed out that the Brazilian had been involved in more on-track collisions than any other world champion. Senna reacted so angrily that he seemed on the point of walking out.

But there was certainly no doubting his commitment. BBC Grand Prix producer Piers Croton recalled his first meeting with the Brazilian at the 1985 European Grand Prix at Brands Hatch. *"It was my first race on-site and I remember Mansell won,"* he told the author. *"Senna asked to view any footage we had of him on track after practice – the day before qualifying, as I recall. I think he must have spent nearly an hour with me looking at different laps but concentrating on the section down from Druids and past the back of the pits – Graham Hill Bend to Surtees. We must have run the videotape back and forth 20 or 30 times as he checked his line."*

Senna's 1991/92 team mate Gerhard Berger saw him as, by nature *"an extremely hardworking and ambitious fellow."* He said: *"That, and his extraordinary ability, perhaps made him unapproachable for many: a supernatural being whom one can't relate to."* But, said the Austrian who became Senna's closest friend in F1: *"In the course of time he became more relaxed. A warm sense of fun developed between us, which really suited him."*

This sense of fun found expression in the notorious practical jokes the two drivers played on each other. On one occasion Berger threw Senna's briefcase out of the helicopter in which they were travelling. It was recovered but in a distinctly battered condition. Senna yelled: *"This is too much. That was a $1,000 briefcase."* Berger was unmoved. *"It's your fault,"* he replied. *"You should have a 50-quid bag like mine."*

Another jape involved doctoring Senna's passport by replacing the picture with a similarly-sized illustration of male genitalia cut from a pornographic magazine. *"It was very cleverly done,"* team co-ordinator Jo Ramirez recalled. *"It caused Ayrton a lot of embarrassment at the first passport control where the officials had to check the passport and there was a considerable delay until the offending picture was replaced."*

Life with Senna wasn't all laughs for Berger. As usual, Senna spent the winter of 1990/91 in Brazil and the Austrian offered to handle all the pre-season testing. But in qualifying for the first race, Senna immediately put the car on pole with Berger third. *"Gerhard was destroyed,"* Ramirez recalled. *"It took him weeks to get to grips with himself again and realise that beating Senna was impossible."* Years after Senna's death Berger recalled: *"He taught me a lot about our sport; I taught him to laugh."*

Like many of his contemporaries Senna enjoyed all-consuming hobbies. Elio de Angelis was an accomplished pianist and Riccardo Patrese was passionate about collecting model trains. Senna liked building and flying model aircraft and became a skilful pilot (see box). Prof Sid Watkins introduced him to fishing and that too became a pastime he enjoyed.

OMP
CIK 118

Ironically, it was when Senna was not a serious title contender that his reputation stood at its highest. In 1989 he was criticised for his impetuosity and ruthless desire to win that transcended everything he did. But in 1993, when he was to some extent the underdog to his old nemesis Prost, his ability shone out even more brightly, particularly when it was wet. His victory at the European Grand Prix at Donnington Park following an electrifying opening lap further embellished the Senna legend. Indeed, that achievement is still fresh in the minds of many F1 followers.

Four times world champion Lewis Hamilton is among them. *"His ability in the rain is something I've aspired to since I've been racing,"* Hamilton said. *"I've always tried to utilise the opportunity to shine and that's what he was able to do. My wet record is pretty good in F1 so I take great pride in knowing that Ayrton was like that too."*

The fact was that, like him or loathe him, Ayrton Senna's presence, in his trademark yellow helmet, added excitement to every F1 race in which he competed. It was a rare quality and one shared with few other drivers.

Following his death there were many tributes to the man from Sao Paulo who had so enlivened F1 during one of the most stirring periods in its history. This was one of the simplest and most heartfelt: on the front page of the issue carrying the report of the fateful San Marino Grand Prix, the Italian magazine Autosprint featured a portrait of Senna with a two-word message -

Addio, Campione.

«

Ayrton Senna in the pits before the Formula One United States Grand Prix in Phoenix, Arizona, 1991

Senna was devastated by the death of Roland Ratzenberger but felt he had to race on at Imola

The Formula 1 world paid tribute to Senna at the next Grand Prix in Belgium

APPENDIX

AYRTON SENNA BY NUMBERS

Senna celebrates a victory, Grand Prix of Germany 1990

C9

When he died, Ayrton Senna sat second on the all-time list of Formula 1 race winners and podium finishes, beaten only by Alain Prost. He did have the accolade for the most laps leading a Grand Prix and the most flag-to-flag victories. Although modern drivers like Lewis Hamilton and Max Verstappen have surpassed many of Senna's totals, helped by a trend towards uncompetitive championship races, Senna's statistical achievements still rank among the best.

SENNA

Born: 21/03/60, Sao Paulo, Brazil
Died: 01/05/94, Maggiore Hospital, Bologna, Italy
Grand prix victories: 41
Pole positions: 65
Fastest laps: 19
World championship points: 614
World championships: Three (1988, 1990,1991)

GRAND PRIX WINS BY SEASON

1985 (Lotus) Portuguese, Belgian
1986 (Lotus) Spain, Detroit
1987 (Lotus) Monaco, Detroit
1988 (McLaren) San Marino, Canada, Detroit, Britain, Germany, Hungary, Belgium, Japan
1989 (McLaren) San Marino, Monaco, Mexico, Germany, Belgium, Spain
1990 (McLaren) Phoenix, Monaco, Canada, Germany, Belgium, Italy
1991 (McLaren) Phoenix, Brazil, San Marino, Monaco, Hungary, Belgium, Australia
1992 (McLaren) Monaco, Hungary, Italy
1993 (McLaren) Brazil, Europe (Donnington), Monaco, Japan, Australia

FI SEASON BY SEASON

Year	Wins	No of races	Poles	Fastest laps	Championship position
1984	-	16	-	1	9th
1985	2	16	7	3	4th
1986	2	16	8	-	3rd
1987	2	16	1	3	3rd
1988	8	16	13	3	1st
1989	6	16	13	3	2nd
1990	6	16	10	2	1st
1991	7	16	8	2	1st
1992	3	16	1	2	4th
1993	5	16	1	1	2nd
1994	-	3	3	-	-

MULTIPLE F1 WORLD CHAMPIONS

Driver	Titles	Champion years
Lewis Hamilton	7	2008, 2014-15, 2017-20
Michael Schumacher	7	1994-95, 2000-04
Juan Manuel Fangio	5	1951, 1954-57
Sebastian Vettel	4	2010-2013
Alain Prost	4	1985-86, 1989, 1993
Ayrton Senna	3	1988,1990-91
Sir Jackie Stewart	3	1969, 1971, 1973
Niki Lauda	3	1975, 1977, 1984
Nelson Piquet	3	1981, 1983, 1987
Sir Jack Brabham	3	1959-60, 1966
Max Verstappen	3	2021-23

ALL-TIME TOP TEN GRAND PRIX WINNERS

Driver	GP wins	Years active in F1
Lewis Hamilton	103	2007-present
Michael Schumacher	91	1991-2006, 2010-2012
Max Verstappen	54	2015-present
Sebastian Vettel	53	2007-2022
Alain Prost	51	1980-1991, 1993
Ayrton Senna	41	1984-1994
Fernando Alonso	32	2001, 2003-18, 2021-present
Nigel Mansell	31	1982-1994
Sir Jackie Stewart	27	1965-1973
Jim Clark	25	1960-68
Niki Lauda	25	1971-1979, 1982-1985

BRAZILIAN WORLD CHAMPIONS

Driver	GP wins	Championships
Emerson Fittipaldi	14	2 (1972, 1974)
Nelson Piquet	23	3 (1981, 1983, 1987)
Ayrton Senna	41	3 (1988, 1990, 1991)

MOST CONSECUTIVE WINS AT THE SAME GRAND PRIX

Driver	Wins	Race	Years
Ayrton Senna	5	Monaco	1989–93
Lewis Hamilton	5	Spanish	2017–21
Juan Manuel Fangio	4	Argentine	1954–57
Jim Clark	4	Belgian	1962–65
Jim Clark	4	British	1962–65
Ayrton Senna	4	Belgian	1988–91
Michael Schumacher	4	Spanish	2001–04
Michael Schumacher	4	United States	2003–06
Lewis Hamilton	4	British	2014–17
Lewis Hamilton	4	United States	2014–17
Max Verstappen	4	Abu Dhabi	2020–23

MOST CONSECUTIVE SEASONS WITH AT LEAST ONE RACE WIN

Driver	Wins	Years
Michael Schumacher	15	1992–06
Lewis Hamilton	15	2007–21
Alain Prost	10	1981–90
Ayrton Senna	9	1985–93
Nelson Piquet	8	1980–87
Max Verstappen	8	2016–23

MOST FLAG-TO-FLAG WINS

Driver	Wins
Lewis Hamilton	23
Ayrton Senna	19
Sebastian Vettel	15

LAPS AS RACE LEADER

Driver	Laps
Lewis Hamilton	5,455
Michael Schumacher	5,111
Sebastian Vettel	3,501
Ayrton Senna	2,932
Max Verstappen	2,858

MOST POLE POSITIONS

Driver	Poles
Lewis Hamilton	104
Michael Schumacher	68
Ayrton Senna	65
Sebastian Vettel	57
Jim Clark	33
Alain Prost	33

MOST POLE POSITIONS IN A SEASON

Driver	Poles	Year
Sebastian Vettel	15	2011
Nigel Mansell	14	1992
Ayrton Senna	13	1988
Ayrton Senna	13	1989
Alain Prost	13	1993

MOST CONSECUTIVE POLE POSITIONS

Driver	Poles	Year
Ayrton Senna	8	1988-89
Ayrton Senna	7	1990-91
Alain Prost	7	1993
Michael Schumacher	7	2000-01
Lewis Hamilton	7	2015
Niki Lauda	6	1974
Ayrton Senna	6	1988
Ayrton Senna	6	1989
Nigel Mansell	6	1992
Mika Hakkinen	6	1999
Nico Rosberg	6	2015
Lewis Hamilton	6	2016

Marlboro
BOSS
Marlboro
HONDA
HONDA
NACIONAL

AYRTON
Marlboro
Shell
BOSS
Ayrton